DOG
Trivia

Judy Doherty
John C. Doherty

Published by Quinlan Press, Inc.
131 Beverly Street
Boston, MA 02114
(617) 227-4870

Cover design by Judy Doherty

Library of Congress Catalog Card Number
85-73127
ISBN 0-933341-25-3

First printing November 1985
Second printing January 1986

DEDICATION

To my favorite canine friend, Bear, who with typical Beardie enthusiasm has trekked many hundreds of miles to go "on with the show."

ACKNOWLEDGEMENTS

We would like to thank the following people for tracking down various information:

Roberta A. Vesley, Library Director, American Kennel Club
Brenda Smith, American Kennel Club Library
Marie Fabrizi, American Kennel Club Library
Connie Allison
Linda Arnette
Carole Bolan
Sharon Lowenthal
Barbara Marshall
Sarah E. Meizlik
Virginia Parsons
Julie J. Treinis
Nora J. Parker, Vice President, St. Hubert's Giralda

Judy Doherty, co-author and illustrator of **Dog Trivia**, attended the Art Center College of Design in Los Angeles, California. She has been active in showing and breeding Bearded Collies and currently is home raising three children and caring for two Bearded Collies, one Cairn Terrier and a Persian cat.

John C. Doherty, husband of co-author Judy Doherty and a graduate of Boston College and Harvard Law School, currently practices law in Boston. He has found dogs to be much more interesting and enjoyable than his fellow members of the legal profession.

Table of Contents

QUESTIONS

GENERAL

1. What famous dog has an AT&T telephone look-alike?

2. What famous Skye Terrier stood vigil over his master's grave for fourteen years?

3. Where is America's oldest canine cemetery located?

4. What famous handicapped woman is credited with bringing the first Akita to the United States?

5. What American order of monks is noted for breeding, raising and training German Shepherds?

6. Would you order an Italian Spinone for dessert?

7. Laika the Spitzlike Russian made history by doing what?

8. What does "Laika" mean?

9. What was the name of America's first Seeing Eye dog?

1

10. What breed is chauffeured by a famous Clydesdale draft team?

11. Is a "Dogger Bank" a place where dogs can have a savings account?

12. What Boxer characteristic makes its name appropriate?

13. If a cowboy says, "Come on, little dogie," is he addressing his canine companion?

14. One of the world's most famous trademarks depicts a dog looking into the horn of a disc phonograph. What company uses this trademark?

15. Name the painting of this dog and phonograph.

16. Who painted this famous picture?

17. What was the dog's name?

18. The artist changed one part of the painting when he sold it. Which part did he change?

19. Who is usually found in the "doghouse" of a yacht?

20. If someone says your dog is "sharp," should you take it as a compliment?

21. Do large or small dogs generally live longer?

22. What tree with a canine-sounding name blossoms with pink or white flowers early in the spring and bears clusters of small red berries in the fall?

23. What do the Campbell kids call their dog?

24. What biblical event is sometimes used to explain why dogs have wet noses?

25. The cover of a Jethro Tull rock album "This Was" pictures the group surrounded by dogs. How many dogs are pictured?

26. For what is the organization Audio Canis noted?

27. If you were in a "dog-eat-dog" situation, would you find yourself at a dog show?

28. What dog is the model for the hood ornament of a Mack truck?

29. A friend tells you that your Collie has a "good stop." Should you be happy about this?

30. What Hungarian breed has a name like a naval officer?

31. In what American state were the oldest dog bones found?

32. What is considered the "Kentucky Derby" of sheep dog events?

33. How is a "dog ear" useful?

34. What famous rock 'n' roll star sang a sad song about "Old Shep"?

35. If someone makes the comment "let sleeping dogs lie," is the person referring to his or her pets?

36. What song askes about the purchase price of a dog in a pet store?

37. What military phrase is used to describe aerial combat between fighter planes?

38. Is a "dog vane" part of a dog's circulatory system?

39. What is a "three-dog night"?

40. The little boy on the Cracker Jacks box has a dog with him. What is this dog's name?

41. What mythical American folk hero had a Moosehound named Elmer?

42. In what part of the year do we have the "dog days"?

43. When Sergeant Preston said "Mush, you Huskies," who was at the head of his team?

44. This 1930s Ohio grandson of Strongheart taught school children safety, had incredible adventures and was the first dog in history to appear on TV. Name him.

45. The Derby is to English horseracing enthusiasts as what is to coursing followers?

46. What dog of the Louisiana Ozarks reputedly had the astonishing ability to understand and respond to languages and to predict the future?

47. When do you know that your dog is truly housebroken?

48. From where did the word "terrier" come?

49. What occurs at the Mass of St. Hubert?

50. Who sings the song "If Dogs Run Free"?

51. Why is Hachiko, a loyal and devoted Akita, honored each year with a solemn ceremony at the Shibuya railroad station in Tokyo, Japan?

52. What is on the cover of the 17th edition of the AKC's "The Complete Dog Book"?

53. What does "fancy" (as in "dog fancy") mean?

54. What does it mean if your bitch is flagging?

55. If you say you're on the "leaky roof" circuit, does it mean you're a carpenter repairing roofs?

56. What popular children's game is named after a rufous-colored dog?

57. What famous British dog trainer likes to say "walkies" to her charges?

58. If your dog has kiss marks, does it mean that it has an ardent fan?

59. What does it mean when someone "puts on the dog"?

60. What's Eukanuba?

61. What country has the most dog racing tracks?

62. What was advertised on the first cover of the **American Kennel Gazette**?

63. What military service group appears on "Evening Parade" with Corporal Chesty VII?

64. If a person has gone "doggo," does this mean he has gone crazy over dogs?

65. This naturalist initially thought his little mongrel Strickeen was stubborn because the dog followed him through the treacherous Alaskan wilds, but he eventually referred to the dog as "immortal." Who was the man?
    a) John Muir
    b) Admiral Byrd
    c) Charles Darwin

66. "Barbie," the famous doll, has a white Standard Poodle for a pet. Can you name him?

67. What dog's name did many people first learn to read?

68. If you call: "My liam, oh where is my liam?" are you an Irish lady who has lost her little boy?

69. In the 1760s, what plagued England?
    a) The Black Death
    b) Rabid dogs in the cities
    c) Too many dogs in the churches

70. What dog food has featured advertisements showing Champions of different breeds with their "top breeder/owners"?

71. If a Sheepdog is "wearing" sheep, does this mean it has a sheepskin coat?

72. On September 26, 1984, the US issued a stamp designating October as National Crime Prevention Month. What is the name of the dog on the stamp, and what is his breed?

73. What brand of shoe uses a Basset Hound as its logo?

74. When a sheepman describes a dog as either "strong" or "weak," to what is he referring?

75. What award is fashioned after an Egyptian statue exhibited at the Metropolitan Museum of Art?

76. What happened to the English Setter Count Noble after he died?
    a) He was buried under a large chestnut tree on his master's property.
    b) He was put in a grave next to his master.
    c) He was stuffed and sent to the Carnegie Museum in Pittsburgh.

77. If you were invited to the Ashley Whippet Invitational, in what sport would you and your dog be participating?

78. If a golfer slices a dog leg, what has he or she done?

79. The Los Angeles Pet Park was inaugurated in 1929 when Kabar the Doberman was buried there. Who owned Kabar?

80. If your dog's wearing culottes, at which end should you be looking?

81. When and where was the first dog show held?

82. What uninvited canine guest performed his astounding feats at a pennant game between the Dodgers and Reds before 50,000 cheering fans?

83. What happened to the owner and his dog after their performance?
    a) The owner was jailed, and the dog was lost.
    b) They were given a baseball signed by the teams.
    c) They were asked to come back for another show.

84. What letter is known as the "dog's letter"?

85. In Edinburgh, Scotland, there is a monument to Sir Walter Scott and his favorite dog. What is the name and breed of this dog?

86. How many German Shepherds does tennis player Ivan Lendl own?

87. Do dogs sweat?

88. What is the Latin phrase for "domestic dog"?

89. What woman, famed for her studies on chimpanzees, also studied the Wild Dogs of Africa?

90. What famous actor and actress spent the six-month British dog immigration quarantine with their dogs on a 120-foot yacht docked in the port of London?

91. Harry Mozely Stevens of Niles, Ohio, created what famous food in the late 1800s?

92. Why do dogs in the Philippines, China, the Sudan, Southeast Asia and in outreach areas of Africa have to be careful?

93. Finish this song verse: "Me and you and a dog named _____."

94. If you encountered a Wolf Pack in North Carolina, what would you see?

95. What band leader never performed without his pet dog?

96. What breed of dog did this band leader always have in hand?

97. Mastiffs guarded the outside of homes while Llasa Apsos guarded the **inside** of homes in what ancient city in the 1100s?

98. Of the eighty-eight known constellations, how many can be called canine constellations?

99. Name these constellations.

100. One hundred and fifty years ago people in England were terrified of getting rabies. According to author Charles Lamb, how could people tell if a dog had rabies?
   a) The dog twitched and chewed the base of its tail.
   b) The dog wagged its tail horizontally or perpendicularly.
   c) The dog snapped at flies.

101. If you're driving behind a Greyhound bus, which way will the Greyhound pictured on the bus be running?

102. What is the only state in the US that requires a dog to be quarantined for 120 days before entering?

103. Was the Society for the Prevention of Cruelty to Animals founded in the US or in England?

104. Which breeds are generally used as guide dogs for the blind?

105. What is the Dysplasia Control Registry called?

106. How can the OFA tell if your dog is dysplastic?

107. How often should you clip your dog's nails?

108. What city imposes the highest fine for not cleaning up after your dog?

109. When a dog is "docked," what has happened?

123. A person who is called a "dog-face" wears what kind of attire?

124. What event took place at the "Bear Garden" in Elizabethan England?

125. If you are referred to as "dog tired," are you fed up with your pet dog?

126. What is a dog's most important greeting action and sign of friendship?
    a) Barking
    b) Tail wagging
    c) Licking a hand

127. What breeds appear on a famous brand of whisky?

128. Where is a dog's "lozenge mark" or "beauty mark" ideally located?

129. If an aviator or astronaut "screws the pooch," what has happened?

130. Who said, "A door is what a dog is perpetually on the wrong side of"?

131. What breed of dog is sometimes referred to as the "hot dog"?
    a) Basset Hound
    b) Dachshund
    c) Weimaraner

132. With whom was Gidget infatuated?

133. What did Kal Kan "salute" at the AKC Centennial Show?

134. What wrestler wears a big leather collar around his neck?

110. According to the **Guinness Book of World Records**, what was the longest life span of a dog, and where did it live?

111. If you are driving next to a Greyhound bus, will the dog pictured on the side be running with you or away from you?

112. Your Sussex Spaniel is "giving tongue." What's it doing?

113. Americans say that a Cairn Terrier should weigh fourteen pounds. What would the British say?

114. Is a sailor "on a dog watch" looking for dogs who might have fallen overboard?

115. What is distemper?

116. What does a tracking dog wear while working?

117. What dog food manufacturer sponsors the "Great American Dog" contest?

118. What shoe company used the dog Tige in its advertising?

119. What will a sheepdog do if his master says, "Walk on"?

120. Ireland honored its native dogs with a set of beautiful stamps. What are the native Irish breeds?

121. What dog is called the "hound of Hades"?

122. What is cynophobia?

135. Are tulip-eared dogs of Dutch origin?

136. Puppies are sightless and deaf at birth. Approximately how many days does it usually take before a puppy's eyes react to light?

137. How many days after birth before a puppy reacts to noise?

138. The Canid or dog family has been around for how many years?

139. What dog is the mascot of the US Marine Corps and Yale University?

140. What sport did Eva Seely pioneer in 1929?

141. What dog food has recently commissioned the beautiful "Performance Art Series" paintings?

142. Which would you use for a health problem: dogbane or wolfbane?

143. What test have Gail Tamases Fisher and Wendy Volhard devised to provide a scientific approach to the understanding of a puppy's behavior?

144. Why wouldn't you pet a dog with zoonosis hydrophobia?

KNOW YOUR BREEDS

1. This dog's name means "lion," but it is often called "the chrysanthemum-faced dog." Name him.

2. If Red Auerbach, ex-coach of the Boston Celtics, said to a crony, "he's a great Dunker," would he be referring to one of his better basketball players?

3. In the United States, this happy-go-lucky vermin-hunting terrier is sometimes referred to as the "Jones Terrier." What is its official name?

4. The Poodle is not generally well-known for its hunting ability, but for what delicacy has it been known to hunt?

5. What dog is named after a country that is now called Zimbabwe?

6. What three breeds are referred to as "the lions who lie down with lambs"?

7. What is the only color combination acceptable for the Welsh Springer Spaniel?

8. In the late 1800s the Germans renamed

this dog "Deutsche Dogge" and consider it the national dog. What is the dog?

9. What dog was considered the drop-eared variety of the Norwich Terrier until 1971?

10. The Latin expression **multum in parvo** describes the Pug admirably. What does it mean?

11. Which breed of dog most closely resembles a lamb?

12. Which one of these breeds is not a member of the Terrier Group?
    a) Miniature Schnauzer
    b) Yorkshire Terrier
    c) Norwich Terrier
    d) Kerry Blue Terrier

13. What now-extinct breed is thought to be the progenitor of many a modern-day Terrier?

14. What large English sheepdog breed can be referred to as "cobby"?

15. A sleuth can be a detective, but it can also be what breed of dog?

16. Are the Giant, Standard, and Miniature Schnauzers three size variations of the same breed?

17. What breed has the Portuguese name Cao de Agua?

18. What is the largest breed in the Terrier Group?

19. Which one of these breeds is not a member of the Working Group?
    a) Welsh Corgi
    b) Portuguese Water Dog
    c) Great Pyreenes
    d) Kuvasz

20. This breed sometimes has "a hole in its head," which is actually a part of its skull only covered with membrane. What is the breed?

21. What is the "hole in the head" of this breed called?

22. What terrier is known as "the white cavalier"?

23. What breed has recently gotten a bad name for itself because it has been used for pit fighting?

24. What dog did the Chukchi Eskimos breed?

25. What dog is known as the "gray ghost"?

26. Except for their size, what two sheepdog breeds are virtually identical?

27. This intrepid terrier has been called "the D'Artagnon of the show ring."

28. How did the Border Terrier get its name?

29. Which color is not acceptable in Great Danes: brindle, fawn, chocolate, blue, black or harlequin?

30. What breed of dog of English origin

17

makes up the two hound packs known as the Kendal Pack and the Dumfriesshire Pack?

31. Why are Tazys famous?

32. What low-set and lumbering spaniel would look lovely against a lemon-and-white backdrop?

33. Clumber Park is located near what forest?
    a) Yosemite
    b) Sherwood Forest
    c) Black Forest

34. The Bosnian Hound is a native of what country?

35. In 1886 this breed was classified at dog shows in England as "Old English Wire-Haired Black-and-Tan Terriers." What do we now call them?

36. What breed is largely responsible for the Brussels Griffon's facial characteristics?

37. Name the two breeds most commonly used for racing.

38. What name do we give the Plum Pudding Dog, Carriage Dog or Spotted Dick?

39 What is the French Bulldog's most distinctive feature?

40. Which one of these breeds is not a member of the Sporting Group?
    a) Irish Water Spaniel
    b) Vizsla
    c) Tibetan Spaniel
    d) Weimaraner

41. Name a large working dog first bred in a Canadian Maritime Province that is famous for rescuing victims of water mishaps.

42. What Swiss dog is called the "Bruno," the "Jura Lancer" and "A'rogovian Dog"?

43. According to the American Standard, what are the acceptable colors for a Sheltie?

44. What is the only native North American toy breed?

45. If you encountered a "lurcher" in your travels in England, would you have met someone who had just spent too much time in the local pub?

46. From where does the "Owcharka" come?

47. What breed is affectionately called "teckel" in both Europe and the United States?

48. What breed originated in the "Lost Valley"?

49. What breed was called "Petit Barbet" for hundreds of years?

50. Which type of Corgi has a tail?

51. What dog used to be known as the Groenandael?

52. Name the dog bred from two dogs rescued from a shipwreck off the Maryland coast in the 1800s.

53. What breed of dog is born completely white and slowly develops black spots?

54. What dog is the progenitor of the Brussels Griffon?

55. Which came first, the Old English Sheepdog or the Bearded Collie?

56. What dog was called the Queensland Heeler?

57. The Brabancon is the smooth variety of what breed?

58. Name the four types of Swiss Mountain Dogs.

59. If you have a harlequin Great Dane, does this mean you have a pet that likes to clown around?

60. What is the Australian aboriginal dog?

61. In 1979, Malta printed a silver coin commemorating the declaration of the National Dog of Malta. What is the National Dog of Malta?

62. What is the German Shepherd called in most countries?

63. What breed is associated with the Bothkennar Kennels?

64. What dog is the Japanese symbol of good health?

65. What breed of dog was kept by both Tutankhamen and Cleopatra in ancient Egypt as a hunting dog?

66.   Describe the Landseer Newfoundland.

67.   What breed was originially bred by the monks at St. Hubert's Abbey in France?

68.   What breed, favored by the nobles of a German Republic, may be a cross of the Bloodhound and a Schweisshund?

69.   What breed of dog did Commodore Perry bring back from Japan to be a pet for Queen Victoria?

70.   What breed, originally from ancient Egypt, did Moslems consider a gift from Allah?

71.   What breed of dog, which is born mute, was kept by the pharoahs of Egypt?

72.   To what does "bandog" refer?

73.   What is the only AKC breed with a black tongue?

74.   What Chinese dog, which the AKC does not recognize, also has a black tongue?

75.   The Basenji is a distinctive little dog with an interesting trait. What is that trait?
   a)   It fastidiously cleans itself like a cat.
   b)   It has retractable claws like a cat.
   c)   Its sound is somewhat cat-like.

76.   What breed of dog cannot receive the title of Champion in Belgium unless it has won in a police, army or defense dog competition?

77. Which one of the Corgis has the closest ties to Schipperkes and Pomeranians?

78. In 1907 Captain John Barff brought "Zardin" to England from Persia. What was Zardin?

79. Which came first, the White Bull Terrier or the Colored variety?

80. What is another name for the German Bulldog?

81. What dogs were registered as Belgian Sheepdogs until 1959?

82. This supposed ancester of the Manchester Terrier is not in the Terrier Group but rather a hound member. What is this dog?

83. What physical characteristic seldom found in terriers did this hound pass on to the Manchester?

84. What dog of Erin is the tallest of the spaniels?

85. Are the Doberman and Miniature Pinchers two varieties of the same breed?

86. Shelties carry a gene for an absence of tan markings in the blues and blacks. The official AKC designations are blue-and-white and black-and-white, but what do Sheltie fanciers call these colors?

87. What can be said about the Xoloitzcuintli?

88. This breed has been called the Waterside, Working and Bingley Terrier. What is it called today?

89. What are American Black and Tan, Bluetick and Redbone's?

90. Descended from greyhounds, the Cirneco Dell'Etna became indigenous to an island and were often used to hunt along the slopes of Mt. Etna. Where is this dog's home?

91. From where do the Puffin dog, Dunker and Haldenstiver come?

92. What dog was reputedly created when a lion "yielded to the caresses of a butterfly"?

93. What dog comes colored in blue, lemon, orange and liver belton?

94. What dog is known as "the Abraham of his breed"?

95. What breed is named after the mountain range separating Spain and France?

96. What breed seldom takes a "sensational stand" and was admired by Daniel Webster?

97. What dogs were originally bred by British miners who crossed Greyhounds with Terriers?

98. Which variety of Saint Bernard is most suited to the snow covered icy climes of the Alps?

99. What dog is called the "little captain"?

100. What else could you call the Papillon and the Phalene?

101. The "lozenge mark" is specific to what two breeds?

102. What American breed of dog is descended from the breedings of Judge to Gyp and Eph to Tobin's Kate?

103. What breed of dog is the only one whose work can be presented as evidence admissible in court?

104. What notorious scavenger dog found particularly in Asia and Africa has never been fully domesticated and is instinctively disliked by other dogs?

105. What breed comes in color mixtures called "roan"?

106. The Canaan Dog has recently been used in Israel for what purposes?

107. Which one of the following three does not wear a "saddle": Lakeland, Welsh or Irish Terrier?

108. What is the African Barkless Dog?

109. What is a Min Pin?

110. In what country did the Shih Tzu originate?

111. What is a rough translation of Affenpinscher?

112. During the 1800s the Saint Bernards at the "Hospice" became depleted because of inbreeding and sickness. An outcross with what breed resulted in a re-invigorated Saint Bernard?

113. Due to crossing, what change occurred in the Saint Bernard?

114. What interchangeable names were given to a short-legged long-coated white dog dating back to 250 BC?

115. What does "basset" mean in French?

116. "The red, long-tailed dog goes at night into the stalls of the hills, . . . his face glows like a God and he delights to do his work." What dog does this describe?

117. What country is the home of the Fila Brazileiro?

118. What happened to the first pair of Basenjis brought to the outside world?
    a) They died of distemper.
    b) They were stolen.
    c) They were unable to reproduce.

119. What dog was known as the Talisman Dog until 1935?

120. The Silky Terrier is basically derived from what two breeds?

121. The Belgian Street Dog was one of the true founders of what breed?

122. What dog could be called "the golden pointer from Hungary"?

123. What three colors are acceptable for Labrador Retrievers?

124. Some people believe that this dog arose "fully formed from among the shamrocks."

125. What breed of dog is the smallest of the Sporting Dogs?

126. In France this dog is called Korthals Griffon. Is it a Brussels or Wirehaired Pointing Griffon?

127. What very rare breed, whose name comes from the French word for beard, is often declared the father of the Poodle and progenitor of many pointing breeds?

128. The lovely Ibizan Hounds come from Ibiza Island. Where is this island located?

129. What country is in love with Fox Terriers?

130. Is it wise to have a Komondor and a Border Collie working a flock of sheep together?

131. What is the Croatian Sheepdog's native country?

132. What dog was originally bred as the "Gamekeeper's Night Dog"?

133. In France, is a "billy club" always considered a short, hard object used as a weapon?

134. If Count Dracula were out hunting for

something other than his favorite en-
tree, what breed of dog would he most
likely take with him?

Complete these breed's names:

135. Affen _____

136. Rodesian _____

137. _____ Malamute

138. Bearded _____

139. Dandie _____

140. Flat-_____ Retriever

141. Golden _____

142. Ibizan _____

143. _____ Chin

144. Kerry _____ Terrier

145. Lhasa _____

146. Doberman _____

147. _____ Elkhound

148. Portuguese _____ Dog

149. _____ Bernard

150. Shetland _____

151. Shih _____

152. Silky _____

153. Soft Coated _____ Terrier

154. American _____ Terrier

155. West _____ White Terrier

156. Wirehaired _____ Griffon

157. Black and _____ Coonhound

158. Bichon _____

159. Cavalier _____ _____ Spaniel

160. _____ Griffon

161. Chow _____

162. Cardigan _____ Corgi

163. Bernese _____ Dog

164. _____ Malinois

DOGS IN HISTORY AND POLITICS

1. Willie the Bull Terrier belonged to what renowned WWII general?

2. What famous Saint Bernard saved approximately forty people in the Alps during the late 1800s?

3. Manfred Von Richthoffen, the famous "Red Baron" of WWI fame, often had his pet dog fly with him. Name this canine co-pilot.

4. What breed of dog was he?

5. Did Lyndon Johnson pick up "Him" or "Her" by the ears?

6. What presidential dog once pilfered the contents of nineteen breakfast plates left unattended in the White House kitchen?

7. In the days of the Roman Empire, if you are visiting a friend's villa and see a sign with the words **Cave Canem,** what should you do?

8. Chips the war dog received the Silver Star (for gallantry) and the Purple

Heart, but he bit what famous WWII general who tried to give him a congratulatory pat on the head?

9. Perites belonged to what great conquerer?

10. This famed American wanted dogs utilized for defense against Indian raids; instead, he was told to go fly a kite. Who was he?

11. What was Peter the Great's Italian Greyhound named?

12. According to Celtic mythology, what dog's paw marks are still imprinted in stone in southern Wales?

13. The first Ken-L-Ration Dog Hero of the Year Award was given in 1954 to what dog?

14. What is the name of President and Mrs. Reagan's new canine addition?

15. If Fidel Castro had gone to battle 300 years ago, would the White Cuban Dog have been at his side?

16. Name the sacred book of the Persians which says a yellow-eared dog guards the rainbow bridge spanning the gap between the lands of the living and the dead.

17. What was the name of the Poodle given to actress Helen Hayes on the gangplank of a trans-Atlantic liner about to depart from England to the United States?
    a) Turvy
    b) Topsy
    c) Puddin

18. American actress Marion Davies held a funeral service—officiated by a priest—for her beloved Dachshund. What was the name of the deceased pet?

19. When King Charles II returned to London from exile in France, the first boat bringing his belongings also brought his litttle pet Spaniel. What was its name?
    a) Cupid
    b) Angel
    c) Eros

20. In what war were dogs officially used by the US military?

21. During what presidential administrations did Airedales reign supreme?

22. King Cormac of Ireland had a great kennel of Irish Hounds in the 4th century. Who was the famed master of these Hounds?

23. What pet of a French-African regiment was smuggled back to Europe in a drum?
    a) Thoutou
    b) Bonjour
    c) Letrec

24. Which US service corps maintained the "Devil Dogs" during WWII?

25. What famous American Revolutionary is said to have representatives of the Briard breed brought to this country?

26. When an Aztec was having a bout with rheumatism, where did he put his handy little Mexican Hairless, hoping for a cure?

27. What was the name of Calvin Coolidge's naughty dog who was banished to Never-Never Land?

28. In 1878, Queen Victoria sent two of what breed of dog over to New York to be entered in the Westminster Kennel Club Show?

29. Calvin Coolidge was born in Northampton, Massachusetts, and later became a governor of Vermont. Among his pet dogs, a prim female white Collie bore what very Yankee name?

30. Among Cal Coolidge's canines was a Sheepdog who used to join the President and his friends for coffee. What was this caffeine-crazed canine named?

31. Although Admiral Byrd used Siberian Huskies on his successful Antarctic expedition, he said he would have preferred using what other breed?

32. What man's mother supposedly dreamed she had barking pups in her belly, "all white and red upon the back"?

33. In Edward II's time (1307-1327) "a rough sort of dog between a hound and a terrier" was used for hunting. What was it?

34. What is Vice-President George Bush's dog named?

35. In what country's legend does King Menes I get attacked by his own hounds, only escaping by fleeing across the water?

36. Clipper the German Shepherd was the favorite of what presidential first lady?

37. During WWII what country used special detachments of dogs trained to detect persons buried in avalanches?

38. The dog was considered the symbol of power on British coinage before what animal took its place?

39. Nixon's dogs Pasha and Vicky met which of Johnson's dogs?
    a) Blanco
    b) Yuki
    c) Him

40. The Lyndon B. Johnsons were fond of their Beagles, but Blanco also resided with them. What breed was Blanco?

41. What emperor sent out this notice: "Lost! Dog 'branded' on right shoulder with the letter 'C.' Please return to Emperor"?

42. The oldest recorded tall-tale about a dog tells of a Mastiff sent to King Cyrus from the King of Albania. He was told the dog wasn't an ordinary cur and should not be used to fight against common creatures like a Persian dog or bull. What did the dog fight in this tall tale?

43. What memorial was made of President Harding's dog, Laddie Boy?

44. What great leader is said to have had hunting expeditions with up to 10,000 dogs in attendance?

45. What traveler reported on these rather ambitious hunting expeditions?

46. What breed of dog is said to have been with Frederick the Great when he hid under a bridge as the opposing army marched overhead during the Seven Years War?
    a) Pug
    b) Great Dane
    c) Italian Greyhound

47. What militaristic knights were "saved in the deserts of Phrygia" because of their hounds?

48. What did the dogs find that made the survival of these men possible?

49. Roman Governor Publius loved his little dog so much he had a painting made of her. To honor the painting and the dog, a poem was written about her. What kind of dog was she?

50. When General Howe's dog wandered into an American camp, this man returned the dog with the following note: "...he does himself have the pleasure to return to him a dog with General Howe's name on the collar...." Who returned the dog?

51. President Carter's daughter Amy and her dog Grits were host and hostess to what famous Broadway canine celebrity?

52. Prince Albert's favorite Greyhound Eos had a silver collar with a mock padlock. How does one open this tricky little device?

53. Yama, the god of death, had the sun-dogs and the moon-dogs guard the kingdom of the dead. What religious group has these figures?

54. How did President Lyndon B. Johnson's dog Him die?

55. What Roman wrote his "Treaty of Hunting" to give justice to the Gallic Hound, who he said were rough-coated and of a savage but sad appearance?

56. What dog of today was he probably talking about?

57. The famous "Hounds of St. Hubert" were.
    a) Red
    b) Brindle
    c) White

58. Blanco was not a good host to a fellow Collie and growled at this canine star visiting the White House. Name the star.

59. With whom was George Washington angry for not taking care of the hounds Lafayette had given to his care?

60. At the court of Louis XIV, the sun king, what breed was referred to as the "gentleman with the white fur"?

61. What was the name of the organization

formed during WWII that supplied some 17,000 dogs to the armed forces?

62. What saint's mother is said to have dreamed she gave birth to a dog with a torch in its mouth?

63. Calvin Coolidge's first White House dog had a nasty habit that got him banished from his home. What was this habit?

64. After the sack of the Summer Palace in Peking, General Dunne of the English Army presented a captive canine to Queen Victoria. What was this little gift's name?

65. Is First Lady Nancy Reagan's new dog a Cocker Spaniel or a Cavalier King Charles Spaniel?

66. What country did George Bush's dog visit when Bush was ambassador?

67. Prior to the French Revolution, what breed of dogs was the favorite hunting dog of the French royal family and aristocracy?

68. What color is the hound on the banner the Prince of Wales used at his investiture ceremonies?

69. Howel the Good, King of Southern Wales, enacted the first known laws concerning dogs. What were they called?

70. What dogs were known to have sported "Imperiales" during the reign of Louis XVI?

71. Queen Elizabeth I is said to have had a

pack of dogs so small you could put one in a "gauntlet glove." What were they called?

72. King Matthias Corvinus of Hungary had many of these dogs in the 13th century, and always kept one at his side. Name this breed.

73. King Henry VIII must have really loved this dog, because a number of rewards were given out "for bringing the King's spanyelle ayen" (i.e., home again). What was the name of this valued little pet?
   a) Cutie
   b) Sweetie
   c) Muffin

74. What did the "M-dogs" do?

75. Why was this team of dogs services discontinued?

76. President Nixon had a Yorkie and a Miniature Poodle. Which was Pasha and which was Vicky?

77. What breed was referred to as a "Baboon" or monkey-faced dog in an Egyptian papyrus dating to the 4000 BC period?

78. What British breed of dog had its tail docked to prove it was a drover's dog, and thus exempt from taxes?

79. Woodrow Wilson had a favored Airedale. What was his name?
   a) Davie
   b) Richie
   c) Mike

80. What breed type has performed "circus acts" in the coliseum since before 79 AD?

81. What presidential dog was banished for a time from the grounds of the White House for too enthusiastically chasing the local squirrel population?

82. The **Molossus** is a well-known Greek sculpture of a dog. What is the breed of this dog?

83. In what city can this statue be found?

84. What was Gertrude Stein afraid would happen to her dog when the Germans occupied the French town in which she lived?

85. What happened to dogs when taken to the Shrine of Vulcan in the Grotto of Mt. Etna in Sicily?

86. What could this have been an early treatment for?

87. In what country was the earliest confirmed domestic dog found?

88. What famous Trojan called Agememnon a "covetous cur" with "greedy eyes of a dog"?

89. What famous presidential dog was brought home from the Aleutian Islands on a US Naval vessel after a presidential trip?

90. What is the name of the dog President Reagan sent to their ranch in California?

91. In British history it is said that when a

nobleman died in battle, his dog's effigy was placed at his side on the sarcophagus. Where was the dog placed if the lord died peacefully?

92. Along with his wife, what governor from New York State is known to have established the Boxer in the US?

93. What president is written about in the book **Dog Days at the White House**?

94. What toy breed is known to have been in Pompeii when Mt. Vesuvius decimated that city?

95. Lafayette brought the so-called Old Virginia Bench-Legged Beagles to what great American?

96. What did Sam—the Irish hound of Olaf, a 10th century Norwegian prince—do when Olaf gave him to his friend Gunnar?
    a) He howled mournfully for days.
    b) He went and lay down at Gunnar's feet.
    c) He left his master's great hall in fear.

97. What Catholic order is known as the "dogs of God"?

98. Originally thought to be a jackal, what god was known as "The Watchdog of the Dead"?

99. What breed of dog is believed to have hidden under the skirt of Mary Queen of Scots when she was executed?

100. What people have the Keeshond as a "national dog"?

101. After whom are these dogs named?

102. What dog is often erroneously named as the lead dog of the Serum Run to Nome, Alaska, that saved that city from an epidemic?

103. What vice-presidential dog was named after a board game?

104. What prohibited serfs from keeping Spaniels and Greyhounds?
    a) Canute Laws
    b) Magna Carta
    c) Law of the Hounds

105. If you owned a Greyhound within ten miles of the royal forest, what did you have to do?
    a) Cut the tendons of the dog at its hock
    b) Keep it tied up
    c) Muzzle it

106. What was the penalty for bringing the dog within ten miles of the royal forest?
    a) The dog was confiscated and became a part of the royal pack.
    b) The owner had to pay ten pence for every mile nearer the forest.
    c) The dog was killed.

107. What dog became the first and only presidential dog to be admitted to AKC field trial records?

108. For what are the dogs Oomiyak, Kayak, Dingo and Targish noted?

109. What happened to Tickle, one of the Byrd expedition's lead dogs?

110. What hound was mistakenly killed by the Prince of Wales because he thought the dog killed his son?

111. What did the Prince of Wales find after he had killed his dog?

112. What can be found at "Beth-Gelert" near Mt. Snowden?

113. Would Admiral Byrd's dog Igloo be pulling the sled or riding in it?

114. Was the hospice of St. Bernard named after the dog of the same name, or was the dog named after the hospice?

115. Name the great wolf-dog of Norse mythology.

116. In 1260 AD the first pack of Harriers were organized. What was the name of this pack?

117. Satan left the body of this betrayer in the form of a dog. Who was he?

118. What presidential dog was named after an estate in Scotland?

119. What Greek goddess is known as "Our Lady of the Hounds"?

120. Morfino, an intrepid pet of an Italian officer in the Napoleonic Wars, traveled hundreds of miles to find his master. What breed was Morfino?

121. What were dogs belonging to the Crusaders supposedly able to do?

122. He was the only dog of the sole litter of Turkish sheepdogs born in this country, and the only dog of this breed to serve in the US Armed Forces. What was his name?

123. What great Celtic dog was highly valued by the Romans?

124. What was the name of Eisenhower's White House dog?

125. What was this dog's breed?

126. The popularity of the Pekingese increased because of what royal lady's love for them?

127. Bonne, Ponne and Nonne were three hunting dogs belonging to what famous king of the 1600s?

128. What New World conquerer used dogs to help him subdue the Indians of Mexico?

129. What famous English king sent 400 Mastiffs to Charles V of Spain to help in his war against France?

130. Seumas the crippled shepherd boy had his Collie Davie taken from him because he was told "a widow wanted the four best Collies in Scotland." Who was the "widow"?

131. The Duke and Duchess of Windsor were enthusiasts of what breed?

132. What religious group is said to have taken Pointers and Foxhounds to their new homes in Utah?

133. What was Moustache, a renowned Poodle hero of the Napoleonic wars, given by the soldiers who idolized him?

134. A German Shepherd owned by Herbert Hoover was named after a very famous Egyptian king. Can you name this regal Shepherd?

135. Herbert Hoover's dog Pat was noted for opening doors in the White House for himself and yet another Hoover dog, a Norwegian Elkhound. Name this Elkhound.

136. Margaret Truman, daughter of President Harry Truman, wrote a book about various presidential menageries. What was the book's title?

137. Two thousand years ago, Plutarch told a story about a poodle-like dog named Zoppico who performed for the Emperor Vespasian. What did this little dog do?

138. The Postmaster General of the United States gave Margaret Truman a dog. What breed was it?

139. While Emperoress Josephine was in prison she sent messages to her husband Napoleon via her little dog. How did she do it?

140. Englishwoman Jean Waring bred minia-

tures and whites of this breed in the '50s, and wrote a little book about them called **The Fluffy Lions, The Story of Mighty Atom, Poppet and Company**. What was the breed?

141. What breed of dog's hair was made into socks during WWI for wounded soldiers?

142. Who was King Timahoe's owner?

143. What breed of dog did Winston Churchill own?

144. What breed's name comes from the Chinese traders' slang for "knick-knack"?

145. Which of these was used as a flea remedy of the 1800s?
    a) Turpentine mixed with soap
    b) Powdered ammonic-chloride of mercury
    c) Powdered pyrethrum roseum

146. Which of the above elements is an ingredient in today's flea remedies?

147. Liberty was whose White House friend?

148. Where did President Johnson get Yuki?

149. Was the "Healing Paw" an early obedience group?

150. What famous saint said he was "saved by dogs" during his escape from captivity in Ireland?

151. Alexander the Great thought so highly of his hound that he had a city named after him. Where was the city located?

152. In the Spanish-American War, this dog wasn't a Rough Rider, but he never led a patrol that was ambushed. Name the dog.

153. What breed of dog barely survived the Chinese Revolution because it was the favorite pet of the despised royalty and therefore was slain by the revolutionaries?

154. What was odd about Anubis, the dog in Egyptian myth?

155. When a reporter made an erroneous statement about George Bush's dog, his owner made a coat for the dog which corrected the mistake. What did it say?

156. What was the wolf-like animal which lived fifteen million years ago and is the ancestor of the modern dog?

157. What activity did WWII vets do as part of a rehabilitation program conducted at Camp Ellis, Illinois?

158. What kind of dogs took part in the rehabilitation program at Camp Ellis?

159. What were these dogs nicknamed?

160. What Greyhound near Lyons in eastern France was made a saint for saving a child's life from a rattlesnake in its cradle?

161. Where did the slaughter of hundreds of thousands of pet dogs and strays occur in the fall of 1983 in order to prevent disease epidemics?

162. If you were caught and accused of the crime of "dog-draw":
     a) Where would you be?
     b) At what period of history would this be?
     c) What would you have done?

163. Which of these people admired Papillions?
     a) Marie Antoinette
     b) Madame de Pompadore
     c) Louis XIV

164. Who said:
     "If a dog will not come to you after he has looked you in the face, you ought to go home and examine your conscience"?

165. The following story has circulated for years: While touring the British Isles, golden-haired Russian circus dogs bred with Bloodhounds and created this breed. To what breed does this tale refer?

166. Alexander the Great imported dogs from India after his conquest and used them in battle against his enemies. What type of dogs were these?

167. "Molossi" were highly valued in Rome as fighting dogs, guardians of towns and participants in gladiator events. What were they?

168. Queen Victoria owned a Pomeranian that won acclaim at a number of dog shows. What was her name?
      a) Mona
      b) Gona
      c) Rona

169. In 1933 the present Queen Elizabeth and Princess Margaret were given a dog named Roseval Golden Eagle by their father. What breed was this dog?

170. Name the Greek god of medicine who as an infant was saved from starvation by suckling a bitch.

171. This Irish Wolfhound was given to the Kennedy family by a Dublin priest. What was his name?
      a) King Conor
      b) Wolf
      c) Finn

DOGS IN ART AND LITERATURE

1. James Herriot had a pampered Pekingese patient. What was his name?

2. In Andrew Wyeth's painting **Distant Thunder**, what is the dog doing?

3. If Edgar Allen Poe had known about his canine namesake's uses, he probably would have enjoyed writing one of his macabre tales about them. Name this dog.

4. A rather new book called **Nop's Trials** is about what breed of dog?

5. Sir Edwin Landseer's well-known painting **Dignity and Impudence** features a sedate Bloodhound and an impudent wheaten Scotch Terrier. Where are they located?

6. Who wrote **Lassie**?

7. Norman Rockwell did a painting called the **Expert Salesman**. How many dogs are pictured, and what kind are they?

8. The sheepdog George had a nameless son who did his job too well. He ran Gabriel Oak's 200 sheep over a cliff to their death. What was the book?

9. What little dogs were part of an entourage of grand ladies in Jane Austen's **Pride and Prejudice**?

10. Who described James Thurber's dogs as looking like unbaked cookies?

11. The two dogs in **The Incredible Journey** were of what different breeds?

12. What were the names of these two canine traveling companions, who also had a feline friend?

13. Which American author said, "If you pick up a starving dog and make him prosperous, he will not bite you. This is the principle difference between a dog and a man"?

14. The famous aristocratic Marlborough family was painted by Gainsborough many times. What kind of dogs are pictured with this family?

15. What author of canine books lived at Sunnybank?

16. In which of James Fenimore Cooper's books does "Hector" play a part?
    a) **The Pioneer**
    b) **Last of the Mohegans**
    c) **The Prairie**

17. Who was Hector's master?
    a) Burberry Jones (alias Longcoat)
    b) Natty Bumppo (alias Leatherstocking)
    c) Jaspar Farweather (alias Clinkscales)

18. In Thomas Eakins' lovely work **Lady with a Setter Dog**, what are the pair doing?

19. What color is the lady's dress?

20. What are the puppies doing in Paul Gauguin's **Still Life With Three Puppies**?

21. Sir Walter Scott's little dog had elegies written to him in English, Latin, French, Italian, Greek, Hebrew, German, Arabic and Hindostanne. What was his name?
    a) Boatswain
    b) Camp
    c) Truffles

22. What author turned down a dinner invitation, apologizing that "the death of a dear old friend"—a dog—kept him from attending?
    a) John Steinbeck
    b) Lord Byron
    c) Sir Walter Scott

23. Rembrandt's paintings contained several of this breed, a cross between Poodle, Spitz and Pinscher. Name the breed.

24. What event prompted William Wordsworth and Sir Walter Scott to write,

and Sir Edwin Landseer to paint?
   a) A dog saving a young child who fell from a cliff into Loch Ness
   b) A dog keeping vigil for three months over the body of its master, who fell from Mt. Helvellyn to his death
   c) A dog defending the battlements of an English fort in Tandoor, India

25. What musician left "the green banks of Shannon" with his "poor dog Tray," and "played a sad lament" when he died at his feet "on a cold winter day"?
   a) The accordian player
   b) The harper
   c) The tin whistler

26. Charles I commissioned Van Dyck to paint five of his children with their canine friends. Where is the large Mastiff located in that picture?

27. Oliver Goldsmith wrote a poem which ended sadly:
>   ...soon a wonder came to light,
>   That shew'd the rogues they lied,
>   The man recovered of the bite,
>   The dog it was that dy'd.

What is the poem entitled?
   a) "An Elegy on the Death of a Mad Dog"
   b) "Sad Tale of a Dog Bitten by a Man"
   c) "The Vicar of Wakefield"

28. Who wrote the following?
An Elegy on a Lap-Dog:
>   Here Shock, the pride of all his kind, is laid;

Who fawn'd like man, but ne'er
like man betray'd.
a) Samuel Pepys
b) Alexander Pope
c) John Gay

29. W.S. Merwin's incredibly sad and poig-
nant poem to one particular dog is actually an anthem to all forgotten and
abused dogs. To whom was this heart-
rending poem dedicated?
a) Allah
b) Ali
c) Omar

30. What beloved dog does John Galswor-
thy refer to as "dog" in his essay "Mem-
ories"?
a) Chris
b) Sonny
c) Worthington

31. What did Buck do at the end of **Call of
the Wild**?

32. Matthew Arnold wrote an elegy called
"At Geist's Grave." What kind of dog
was Geist?
a) Bulldog
b) Dachshund
c) Pug

33. In Edgar Lee Master's **Spoon River An-
thology**, Benjamin Pantier writes that
his dog is his "constant companion,
solace and friend" in his own epitaph.
What was his name?
a) Nip
b) Nig
c) Nit

34. Author George Sand owned a carriage driven by champagne-colored ponies, but instead of a green-coated groom occupying the rear seat, Sand had what sitting beside her?

35. **101 Dalmatians** was based on an actual Dalmatian breeding resulting in fifteen puppies. Who were the mother and father?

36. Tiepolo's **The Dancing Dogs** features four dogs dancing on their hind legs. How many are dressed in coats?

37. What was King Arthur's dog's name?

38. Veronese's **The Marriage Feast of Cana** featured two hounds leashed together. What is this twosome meant to represent?

39. In **Call of the Wild**, Buck battles which dog to gain leadership of the sled team?

40. The Celts have a fairy tale about a very clever "russet dog," but is this devious fellow really a dog?

41. What artist designed the AKC Centennial Commemorative Dog Stamps?

42. In Maud Earl's painting **Silent Sorrow**, for whom is the Wire Fox Terrier "Caesar" mourning?

43. Pierre Auguste Renoir painted **Madame Charpentier and her Children**. What is happening to the dog?

44. What kind of dog is in the painting?

45. In what Joseph Wambaugh book was Vickie the showdog dognapped?

46. What "king of lies and extravagances" described his Greyhound Diana as "running so fast and being in his service so long that she wore her feet down to above her ankles, so in old age she could only be used as a Terrier"?

47. Richard Adams wrote **Watership Down** and **Shardik**. What was the name of his third novel?

48. In Robert Calder's 1976 novel **The Dogs**, what was the name of the laboratory-bred escapee who becomes the leader of a pack of strays?

49. Where is the original of the **Highland Tod Hunter** located?

50. At what was famous English painter Benjamin Marshall expert?

51. F. Scott Fitzgerald mentioned what breed of dog in his writings several times?

52. In **Madeline's Rescue**, what does Genevieve the Poodle do to make all of Miss Clavel's young ladies happy?

53. **Lad: A Dog** was written by whom?

54. Name Jacqueline Susanne's novel about her black Poodle.

55. In the Old Testament's Exodus, how did the Egyptian's dogs help the Hebrews flee?

56. Who has been dubbed the "Miss Manners" of dogs?

57. What breed of dog appears in Carl Sandburg's poem "Dan"?

58. Where can the carvings of **Mahut**, **Abaker**, **Kani** and **Tekar** be found?

59. What color is the little Spaniel in Titian's painting **Venus of Urbino**?

60. John Steinbeck's big "Bleu Poodle" understood "a little Poodle-English," but he responded to what language more quickly?

61. What famous actress wrote the book **Pet Love**?

62. What famous author owns two Great Danes named Juno and Junia?

63. What was Dora's dog named in Charles Dickens' **David Cooperfield**?

64. In the painting **Highland Tod Hunter** by Richard Ansdell, how many dogs with spots are there?

65. Who wrote **Old Yeller**?

66. What was the title of James Thurber's book depicting the strange frustration of several dogs?

67. In Velazquez' painting **Las Menenas**, there is a large dog in the foreground. What's happening to the dog?

68. **Faithful Ruslan** is a story of a dog who:
    a) herds sheep in Hungary.
    b) is a displaced guard dog of a gulag.
    c) guides his blind mistress across the Russian borders to her family in Poland.

69. An unknown author described this breed of dog as "being about the size of a small melon with a tail adorned with a tuft of blond hair." The author also states the dog can be found "in Austin, San Antonio and in tamales, the latter being a Mexican dish, the ingredients of which are as uncertain as those of hash." Name the breed.

70. In the book **The Plague Dogs**, the smaller dog escaped with something on his head. What was it?

71. Charles Dickens had a White Cuban. What was his name?

72. Maud Earl's large painting **Four by Honors** is of what breed of dog?

73. This writer's dog was buried under his master's front door with his portrait and the inscription "Sleep soundly, Maida, at your Master's door above." Name the writer.

74. In Proverbs 5:29 there are four things "which are stately in their ways": the Lion, the Ram, and the King are three. What is the fourth?

75. Winslow Homer did a fine painting called **The Hunter**. What kind of dogs does he have with him?

76. Issa is more frolicksome than Catulla's 'Swallow'
Issa is purer than a dove's Kiss.
Issa is gentler than a maiden,
Issa is more precious than Indian gems,
Lest the last days that she see light should snatch her from him forever,
Publius has had this picture painted.
Who wrote this poem?

77. In the the book **Lassie Come-Home** what did Lassie do for four years at approximately 4:00 p.m.?

78. What was the name of Lord Byron's dog?
a) Tall Boy
b) Boatswain
c) Sailor

79. Lord Byron's beloved dog was of what breed?
a) Pointer
b) Fox Terrier
c) Newfoundland

80. After having one of his terrible fights, James Thurber's dog returned home. Two of his masters were there. What did he do after waiting an hour to greet his third human friend?

81. What is the name of the poem written by Frances Thompson in which God is portrayed in an allegorical fashion as a canine?

82. How did Ernest Hemingway come to own his favorite pet "Alaskan" Springer Spaniel?

83. What "dog" did Robert Frost like to go out and see at night?

84. This Charles Dickens dog was as ill-tempered as his wicked owner and likely to bite his master's boots when he wanted. Name the dog.
    a) Jip
    b) Bull's Eye
    c) Pippin

85. After William Sikes hanged himself in **Oliver Twist**, what did his dog do?

86. Mid-18th century poet Walter Savage Landor loved his little white Pomeranian dearly, and allowed the dog to sit on his head and supervise all he wrote. What was the dog's name?
    a) Giallo
    b) Pomero
    c) Romance

87. Why did the dog's master send him into the river after a stick in Thomas Hardy's poem "The Mongrel"?

88. In James Hardy's painting **A Huntsman with his Deerhounds**, what color are the dogs?

89. In the Fantasy Award-winning novel **City**, dogs inherited the earth. What do the dogs believe about Man?

90. Who said, "But was there ever a dog that praised his fleas"?

91. What author wrote in his **Diary** about King Charles II playing with his dog in the Council Chamber?

92. This earthy American writer said his dog "Tylie Eulenspiegel" haunted his house after her death, meaning he missed her. Who was he?
    a) John Steinbeck
    b) William Faulkner
    c) Ernest Hemingway

93. What were the names of Sir Walter Scott's Greyhounds, who had the interesting habit of jumping in and out of windows?
    a) Lolly and Bear
    b) Judith and Juno
    c) Douglas and Percy

94. Set, the Egyptian god of evil, is often depicted in drawings and sculpture with a dog. What type of dog could it be?

95. What famous poet had a biography written about her as seen through the eyes of her dog Flush?

96. What was the book's name, and who wrote it?

97. Who said "Mad dogs and Englishmen go out in the mid-day sun"?

98. What breed is depicted in Sir Edwin Landseer's **A Distinguished Member of the Humane Society**?

99. White Fang had been trained as a sled dog, but his hated owner made him do what?

100. What happened to the little Smooth Terrier in E.B. White's **A Boston Terrier** after he'd had his "Stone Supreme" awhile?

101. This classic children's book features a young canine who is always late. What is the name of this dog?

102. What canine part is included in the children's rhyme "What Are Little Boy's Made Of"?

103. What legendary Ulster folk hero dedicated himself to serve as the hound of a man named Cullen after killing this man's dog?

104. Who wrote the 14th century book **Traite de la Chasse (A Treatise on Hunting)**, which is probably one of the first detailed books on hunting with dogs?

105. Who coined the phrase "raining cats and dogs"?

106. In Sir Walter Scott's novel **Guy Mannering**, a fellow had some "mustard and pepper" dogs. Who was the man?

107. Who is the heroine of Beatrix Potter's **The Pie and the Patty Pan**?

108. What kind of dog was in Dashiell Hammett's **Thin Man** books?

109. In what book did two sheepdogs keep their master's flock together for four days after their master was bitten by a rattlesnake?

110. In Rembrandt's **Self-Portrait in an Oriental Costume with a Dog**, how is the dog clipped?

111. Eadweard Muybridge was noted for his human locomotion photos, but he did do extensive work with animals. What three breeds did he work with?

112. Which was the white bitch?
   a) Maggie
   b) Lois
   c) Whitie

113. What's her breed?

114. Robert Frost wrote a poem about this Dalmatian who paid him an intrusive visit. Name the poem.

115. Who was Ernest Hemingway's faithful Spaniel companion for twelve years in Cuba?

116. Emmanuel de Witte specialized in authenticity. In his painting **The Interior of the Oude Kerk, Delft**, dogs are sitting, dogs are standing. What is one dog doing?

117. What was the name of Stephen King's novel about a Saint Bernard gone mad?

118. Name the dog in **The World According to Garp**.

119. What were the names of the dogs in **The Plague Dogs**?

120. The tawny Bulldog named Tartar in Emily Bronte's book **Shirley** was actual-

ly Emily's own dog. What was his name?

   a) Keeper
   b) Talbot
   c) Sargeant

121. The Dog Museum of America has exhibited a large statue of a Mastiff. What is her name?

   a) Juno
   b) Queen
   c) Rulfa

122. What Sherlock Holmes mystery features baying dogs?

123. What were the names of Gertrude Stein's Poodles in France?

124. What was the name of James Thurber's childhood dog, an American Bull Terrier?

125. In Andrew Lang's **The Dog of Montargis**, what did the slain master's dog do?

126. The painting **St. Jerome in His Cell** by V. Carpaccio contains a dog. What modern breed does this dog closely resemble?

127. Alfred A. Knopf, the publisher, chose what breed of dog after which to name his books?

128. John Steinbeck's book of his cross-country adventures with his favorite dog was called **Travels with Charley**. What was Charley's complete name?

   a) John Charles

b) Charles le Chien
c) Steiny

129. Which Greek god chose the dog over all the animals on Earth as his own?

130. What long-dead Dachshund companion did E.B. White write about from his hospital sick bed?
a) Fred
b) Raffles
c) Mac

131. What is the name of the protagonist in Beth Brown's **All Dogs Go to Heaven**?

132. Who wrote the Latin work **Of English Dogges, the diversities, the names, natures and the properties**?

133. What great bard spoke of the dogs Trey, Blanch and Sweetheart?

134. In what famous tale did Petticru use his magical powers to make a person forget his sorrow?

135. Who painted **Fighting Dogs Getting Wind**?

136. In **The Book of the Dun Cow**, Chauntecleer the Rooster did his morning crowing from this dog's "sad and lumpy back." What was his name?

137. To whom did James Herriot dedicate his book **All Things Wise and Wonderful**?

138. What famous author received Woggs the Skye Terrier as a wedding gift in August of 1880?

139. What author had a little French Bulldog named Pelleas, and wrote about him in his essay "On the Death of a Little Dog"?

140. The Pekingese Suzi and Chuli belonged to what famous author of children's stories?

141. Alexander Pope's dog had a ball playing with his fancy friend "Fop." What was the dog's name?

142. Which of Chaucer's Canterbury pilgrims showed devotion to "smale houndes"?

143. What does "Queenie" receive as a gift in Truman Capote's **A Christmas Memory**?

144. What geographic barriers blocked Lassie's 400-mile trip to her home in Yorkshire from Scotland in **Lassie Come-Home**?

145. What dogs are pictured in John Sargeant Noble's painting **Untitled**?

146. The little Pug in Goya's painting **The Marchioness of Pontejos** has on a charming little collar. What is on the collar?

147. The dog Aileen Mavoureen reminds one of the story of Gelert in that she saved a child from danger. What American writer of young boy's antics wrote **A Dog's Tale**?

148. How did Abraham Lincoln refer to the character of the dog which appears in

the verses of his poem "The Bear Hunt"?
   a) Feisty
   b) Foxy
   c) Fice

149. In what new novel does Edward the Welsh Corgi have a canine nervous breakdown?
   a) **The Accidental Death**
   b) **The Accidental Meeting**
   c) **The Accidental Tourist**

150. Sir Edwin Landseer did a little painting of a Cairn Terrier. What's he resting his head on?

151. How many dogs are pictured in **The Highland Tod Hunter**?

152. Emily Dickinson wrote that her dog was one of three companions who "knew, but did not tell." Who was the canine companion?

153. William Faulkner described this dog in **The Bear** as part Mastiff with Airedale, some thirty inches at the shoulder, and the color of a "blued gunbarrel." What was his name?
   a) Gun
   b) Lion
   c) Old Ben

154. The Duchess of Alba's 1795 portrait shows a little white dog standing with her. What does he have on his left hind leg?

155. Since 1888 there has been a painting on exhibit at the Royal Academy represent-

ing an event that took place outside King's College Hospital. What was that event?

156. Where is the dog located in Pieter Bruegel's painting **Peasant Wedding**?

157. Philo Vance recognized a runaway Scottie as a dog of high quality, and eventually identified her through AKC records. What was her name and the name of the book?

158. What was the name of Raggedy Ann's dog?

159. In **Peter Pan**, everyone got to fly off to Never-Never Land except the family dog. What was her name?

160. In Ford Madox Brown's allegorical painting **Work**, a Whippet in the foreground is wearing a coat. What color is the coat?

161. White Fang belonged to Gray Beaver, but because of his owner's weakness for the bottle, he was eventually turned over to a despicable white man. What was this man's name?

162. How many Hounds are in Albrecht Durer's engraving **St. Eustace**?

163. Rosa Bonheur was famous for the painting **The Horse Fair**, but the artist also did a painting called **Barbero after the Hunt**. What is painted on the wall next to the dog's chain?

164. In the painting **The Painter and His Pug**, William Hogarth is pictured with one of his Pugs. What was the dog's name?
    a) Heather
    b) Trump
    c) Tara

165. Who wrote **Silver Chief, Dog of the North** and **Valiant, Dog of the Timberline**?
    a) Admiral Richard Byrd
    b) John S. O'Brien
    c) Sydney Le Poir

166. How did Thomas Hardy's dog Moss die?
    a) He was run over by a carter.
    b) He was beaten to death by a tramp.
    c) He died of old age.

PHOTOS

1. If the Gillette Razor Company was looking for a dog to feature in its commercials, it might use this dog. What breed is
   this dog?

2. Who is this handsome fellow, and why
   does he have the good fortune to be pictured in this publication?

Photos

3. What is the name of the dog in the foreground with his paws crossed?

4. What did he do that makes him famous?

5. What was the name of the great dog team driver who ran this dog's famous team?

6. What is the name of this leading animal shelter in Madison, New Jersey?

7. What woman was responsible for founding this non-profit organization devoted to animal welfare?

8. What saint is depicted in the statue in the foreground?

9. Who is the man holding these dogs?

10. What kind of dogs are they?

11. To what World War II organization did he give his dogs?

12. What is the name of this famous movie canine?

13. What movie is this still from?

14. What is the little boy's name in this movie?

15. What actor played him?

16. What is the name of this award?

17. After what "triple crown" winner of the Westminster Kennel Club Show is it modeled?

18. What company commissioned this bronze statue?

19. What is the name of this canine?

20. Who are his human co-stars?

21. Who wrote the **Thin Man** books?

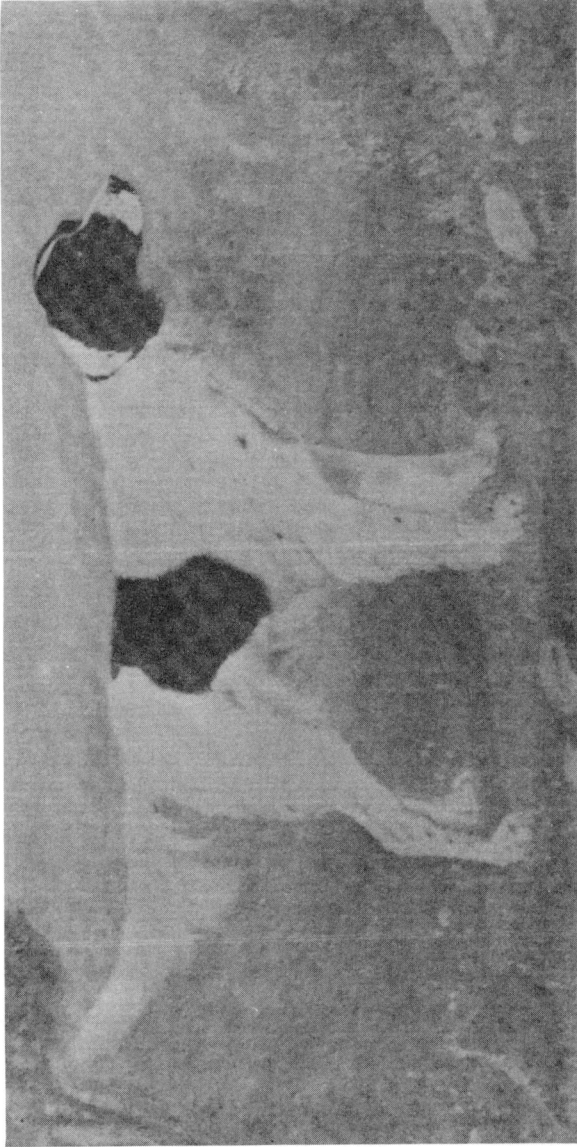

22. What is this dog's breed? 23. What is his name? 24. Why is he famous?

25. After being abandoned by the retreating German Army during World War I, this dog was brought over to the United States, where it became a movie star. What was its name?

26. From what movie was this scene taken?

27. In what year did this dog die?

28. We know who this famous canine star is; who is his lovely co-star?

29. What is the name of the movie?

30. Who is the trainer of this famed dog?

31. What breed is this dog?

32. This breed variety is named after the painter who depicted the breed in his painting **A Distinguished Member of the Humane Society**. Name the breed variety.

33. What makes this breed's feet useful in water?

34. Can you name this TV dog?

35. On what TV show did he appear?

36. Who is the man with him in the photo?

37. What famous American appears with his dog in this statue?

38. Where is this statue located?

39. What is the statue meant to symbolize?

Photos

40. What is this place?

41. Where is it located?

42. Who is the director of this organization?

43. What breed is this?

44. What is the long-haired, black version of this breed called?

45. What is the short-haired type called?

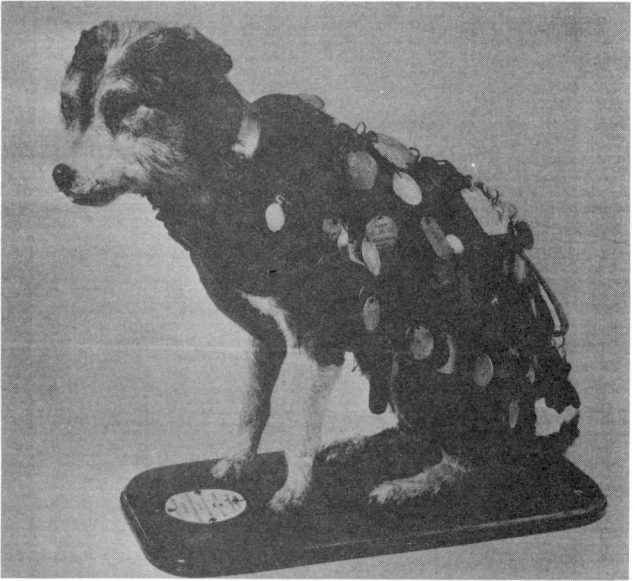

46. What is the name of this little dog?

47. What is his official title?

48. Why is he famous?

49. What is this Obedience trial exercise called?

50. Can you identify the three breeds in the foreground?

51. Name this presidential pair.

52. Which president's dogs were they?

53. Which Soviet leader gave the little white dog to the US president?

54. What event took place between this pair?

55. What breed is the dog on the left?

56. What breed is this dog?

57. What fairy tale name does she have?

58. For what is she noted?

59. Identify this high-flying breed.

60. If you know **Star Wars'** Chewbacka's alien species, you'll know this dog's name.

61. What are this dog and her handler doing?

62. Can you guess this dog's breed?

63. If you're really good, you'll know her name and her impressive titles.

64. What is this breed?

65. This dog is almost certainly related to what massive Russian herdsman's dog?

66. How would you describe this dog's coat?

Photos

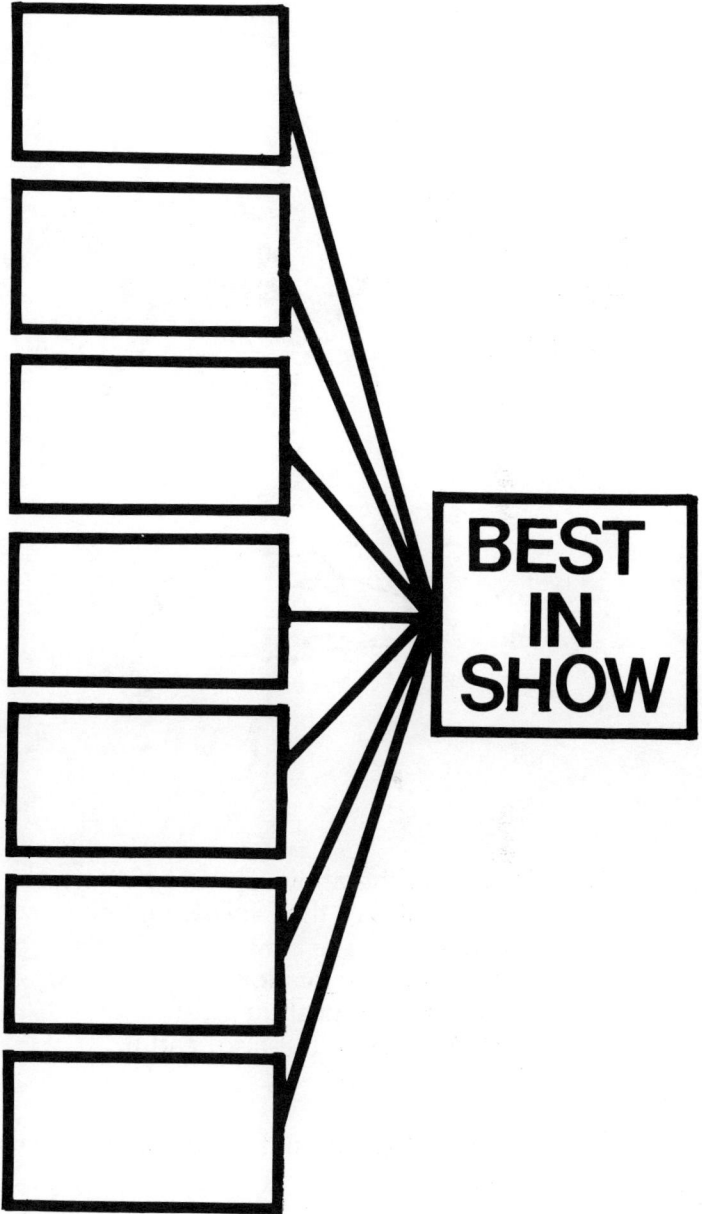

67. Fill in the boxes with the name of the
    seven Groups that will compete for
    "Best in Show."

91

68. Based on the above illustrations, which dog exhibits the following characteristics?
    a) Strong aggression
    b) A fearful posture
    c) Aggressive but also fearful demeanor

69. Which dog should you take most seriously?

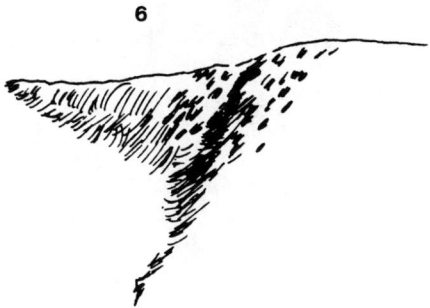

70. The following tail types are illustrated by
the drawings above. Match the tail type
with the drawing.
    a) Fox-brush with sickle curve
    b) Tail with frou-frou or pompom
    c) Docked tail
    d) Gay tail
    e) Ringed tail
    f) Plumed tail

71. The following ear types are illustrated by the drawings below. Match the ear types with the drawings.
    a) Cropped ear
    b) Hanging ear
    c) Bat ear
    d) Prick ear
    e) Button ear
    f) Semi Prick ear

72. Which Poodle has the English Saddle clip, and which has the Continental clip?

73. Name a third Poodle clip in which the Poodle may be shown non-competitively?

74. Name the varieties of Poodles.

75. What Poodle color is also a kind of fruit?

MEDIA DOGS

1. What is the name of the dog in "The Little Rascals"?

2. What famous Cairn Terrier survived a Kansas tornado?

3. Did Old Yeller die of rabies?

4. Superman's dog had a name similar to the planet where Superman was born. Can you name him?

5. What breed of dog is Lady, in **Lady and the Tramp**?

6. Roy Rogers' horse was named Trigger. What was the name of his dog?

7. What are the real names of the dogs in the **Incredible Journey**?
   a) Buffy and Tinker
   b) Tuffy and Link
   c) Muffey and Rink

8. What Walt Disney movie featured more dogs than you would care to feed?

9. What was the name of the talking dog on "The People's Choice"?

10. What breed was this canine star?

11. What breed of dog was the family pet on the soap opera "Ryan's Hope"?

12. The dog which appeared in "The Monroes" was named after a type of winter weather. What was its name?

13. What was the 1972 Dustin Hoffman film which was directed by Sam Peckinpah?

14. What was the name of the "little dog lost" in the movie of the same name?

15. What cartoonist draws "Ben the Hunting Retriever"?

16. The dog in "The Little Rascals" has a circle around which eye?

17. What was the name of the faithful dog in "Land of the Giants"?

18. What was the name of the sheepdog in the TV series "Please Don't Eat the Daisies"?

19. What was the name of the dog in "Nanny and the Professor"?

20. What dog appeared on the short-lived TV series "The Ropers"?

21. "The Partridge Family" had a dog with a French name. What was the name of this dog?

22. What was the name of the family dog in "I Dream of Jeannie"?

23. Name the bionic canine companion of "The Bionic Woman."

24. What breed of dog was this bionic canine?

25. What was the name of the canine cast member of "The Ghost and Mrs. Muir"?

26. What spice shares a name with a dog appearing on "Shirley"?

27. Which popular TV series devoted a special two-hour episode to a dog show?

28. What canine star in this TV episode reportedly has a repertoire of over 270 tricks?

29. What dog appeared in the Tony Curtis movie **Wild and Wooly**?

30. Name the misguided lead in Walt Disney's **The Hound That Thought He Was a Raccoon**.

31. Name the bear in **Old Yeller** that became a friendly playmate of the canine star during the course of filming.

32. Name the prehistoric "dog" in "The Flintstones."

33. Does "Muppets" pup Rowlf have pointed or floppy ears?

34. What TV series had a canine ghost?

35. What was the name of this canine ghost?

36. What did he like to drink?

37. What was the real name of this special dog?

38. What was the name of the dog in the Nestle commercial?

39. What was the name of the dog on "My Three Sons"?

40. In the TV show "Lassie," who was Lassie's first boy owner?

41. Who was Lassie's second boy owner?

42. What was the movie Lassie's original name?

43. What was the locale of the "Rin Tin Tin" TV show?

44. What was the name of the little boy who took care of Rinty?

45. In what state did **Old Yeller** take place?

46. TV waif "Punky Brewster" has a pet Golden Retriever. What is this dog's name?

47. In what post-nuclear war movie does a youth talk to his dog telepathically?

48. George Booth's cartoons are a commentary on the man-dog relationship. What breed does he like to feature?
    a) Bull Terriers
    b) German Shepherds
    c) Beagles

49. The dog who played Old Yeller in the Disney movie was snapped from the

jaws of death at a local pound. What was his name?

50. Name Greg, Peter, Bobby, Jan, Cindy and Marsha's dog.

51. In the comic strip "Johnnie Quest," what was the dog's name?

52. What street waif of comic strip and Broadway fame owned Sandy?

53. Into what did Cinderella's fairy godmother turn Cinderella's dog?

54. What comic strip characters have a dog named Daisy?

55. Ol' Bullet was the dog in what comic strip?

56. What breed of dog is featured in the cartoon strip "Beetle Bailey"?

57. Who was Doggy Daddy's dog child?

58. What did Fred McMurray turn into in **The Shaggy D.A.**?

59. What is the name of the famous comic strip Basset Hound?

60. Ruff appears in what comic strip that features a mischievous little boy?

61. What is the name of the dog in the "Adam" comic strip?

62. What is "Marmadukes's" breed?

63. What was the name of the dog in the "Jiggs and Maggie" comic strip?

64. Name Charlie Brown's famous canine companion, and his breed.

65. In the cartoon "Inspector Gadget," the bumbling inspector has a niece named Penny. What's the name of Penny's dog?

66. Where are Snoopy's markings?

67. What is the name of Snoopy's brother?

68. What breed of dog did Zeppo Marx own?

69. What was Fess Parker and Dorothy Maguire's movie dog?

70. Does Barkley of "Sesame Street" have a long or short coat?

71. Name the Sheepdog from the "Doris Day Show" that was named after a famous British naval hero.

72. What breed starred in the **Return to Oz**?

73. What little TV dog wandered from family to family in each episode helping out wherever he could?

74. Name the robot dog in **Battlestar Galactica**.

75. What was the name of the Jetson family dog in the TV cartoon series?

76. Name Garfield's canine friend.

77. Who is the "world's ugliest dog," according to the Saturday morning cartoons?

78. What does this dog wear on his head so people will not run away in fear and disgust?

79. Name the Walt Disney movie about an Irish Setter.

80. What dog of the afternoon cartoon circuit can turn himself into a vampire bat?

81. What creature does the cartoon character "Fang Face" become on the night of the full moon?

82. Who is the dog in the comic strip "Family Circus"?

83. What was Walt Disney's dog version of Romeo and Juliet?

84. Who is "Hagar the Horrible's" canine friend?

85. In the Masterpiece Theater series "The Irish R.M.," the Royal Magistrate loved to hunt. What was the breed of this gentleman's rather spirited bird dog?

86. What was the name of the Irish R.M.'s dog?

87. What was Betty Boop's dog named?

88. What two dogs appear in "Tom and Jerry"?

89. What breed are these two dogs who terrorize Tom?

90. What 1975 film starring Al Pacino has a reference to "dog" in its title?

91. Name Tom Terrific's dog.

92. Name Sarge's dog in "Beetle Bailey."

93. What is the distinctive facial feature of the Sarge's dog?

94. What type of dog is Scooby-Doo?

95. How are Scooby-Doo and Scrappy-Doo related?

96. Movie star Jean Harlow owned what breed of dog?

97. Name the airborn canine of Saturday morning TV fame.

98. Name Walt Disney's cartoon dog not known for his smarts.

99. What dog made Yosemite National Park a favorite haunt?

100. Who was the Yosemite dog's best friend?

101. What was the name of the little dog that starred with Robert Wagner and Stephanie Powers in the TV series "Hart to Hart"?

102. What is the name of Snoopy's female canine friend?

103. In the movie **Road Warrior**, what type of dog does Mad Max have?

104. What does Mad Max's dog wear around its neck?

105. Dr. Doolittle talked to what dog the most?

106. Edna Ferguson, of the TV soap "All My Children," carries her little "baby" with her all the time. What is this little canine's name?

107. This noted TV personality, who is often a commentator for the Westminster Dog Show and author of over forty animal and dog books, was recently awarded an honorary Doctor of Laws degree at the University of Pennsylvania. Name him.

108. What children's TV cartoon starred "Petey" the puppy?

109. What dog starred in **Silent Call** and **Brawn of the North**?

110. What is the name of the little hound dog in Walt Disney's cartoon movie **The Fox and the Hound**?

111. What dog genius has a time machine?

112. What was the name of the dog in the TV show "The Beverly Hillbillies" and what was his breed?

113. What famous dog changed his name from Higgins and was seen on TV commercials before his big break as a film star?

114. What Walt Disney dog became popular at the beginning of the space age and was appropriately named after a planet?

115. What is the name of the dog that travels **Back to the Future** in the recent movie of the same name?

116. The book and Disney movie **Love Leads the Way** features the story of a faithful and courageous dog. Name this dog.

117. What movie starring Christopher Walken portrayed mercenaries who roamed the world selling their services to the highest bidder?

118. What is unusual about "Dinky Dog"?

119. In the 1930s, MGM Studios made a number of movies called the "All-Barkies" movies. Name the two principal stars.

120. Name the little female dog that dresses up in a cheerleader's outfit in the cartoon series "The Get Along Gang."

121. Lady and the Tramp had four puppies—three took after Mom and one after Dad. Name Tramp's son.

122. Poor-sighted Mr. Magoo has a floppy-eared friend possibly of the hound persuasion. What ancient Roman leader has the same name as Mr. Magoo's dog?

123. What is the name of the family pet in "Bachelor Father"?

124. What cartoon dog is portrayed as a western law enforcement official?

125. Otis Lee, the leader of the Cabbage Patch Kids, patrols the Cabbage Patch with his trusty dog. Name this dog.

SHOW DOGS

1. You read about Ch. Limp-Along of Toady Acres, CD, TDX, in the newspaper. What awards has this dog received?

2. If you went to Crufts, where and what would you be doing?

3. What is a benched show?

4. What man, who held the AKC's first superintendent's license, is known as "Mr. Dog Show"?

5. Should you be worried if your obedience dog has three legs?

6. What dog show, held from 1927 to 1957 at Geraldine Rockefeller Dodge's New Jersey estate, has been considered the most elegant show in America?

7. Name the "once in a lifetime" dog which won the National Amateur and National Open Retriever Championships in 1968, the only time it's ever been done.

8.   In field trials, what is a "brace"?

9.   What are you doing when you make a courtesy turn?

10.   What state was the first to hold obedience tests at an all-breed show?

11.   What was the first obedience club to become a member of the AKC?

12.   Field trials are divided into how many categories?

13.   What are those categories?

14.   You've just received your premium list in the mail. What have you got?

15.   How many points are required for a Field Championship?
        a) Fifteen
        b) Ten
        c) Twelve

16.   What kind of dog is the best tracker?

17.   If you ever referred to a judge at a dog show as a "dogberry," would the judge take this as a compliment?

18.   According to AKC regulations for a TDX Test, the tracking dog must find personal articles of the tracklayer. Which of the following wouldn't be appropriate for this test: a belt, a wallet, socks or eyeglasses?

19.   What is Scent Discrimination as required in an Obedience Utility Class?

20. What breed was the first AKC triple champion?

21. What event was moved in 1979 from the Utility Class in obedience trials to a separate event with its own title and certificate?

22. When can you teach a puppy to track?

23. Who founded the Stewards Club of America?

24. What have you accomplished in order to receive the Green Ribbon?

25. Who was the first woman to judge Best in Show at Madison Square Garden?

26. In field trials and conformation shows, Beagles are divided into two maximum height divisions. What are they?

27. What categories of English Toy Spaniels are accepted for AKC showing?

28. What is the sole difference between Manchesters (other than size), and a show ring disqualifier for the Toy?

29. Who is the "agent" in a dog show catalog?

30. What new group has been added as an AKC dog show category?

31. When heeling your dog in an obedience trial, on which side should the dog be standing?

32. What is an Australian "petrol champion"?

33. How many points are needed to make an AKC champion?

34. When showing your dog in the ring, on which arm should you wear your entry number?

35. What are L's, triangles and T's?

36. What Doberman Pinscher won the Westminster Kennel Club Show two years in a row?

37. How many groups compete for Best in Show?

38. The first three dogs to receive AKC Obedience Championships were of the same breed. Name the breed.

39. What is a Dual Championship?

40. What breed has the most Dual Championships?

41. Into what three categories are Cocker Spaniels divided for show purposes?

42. Where and when did the first North American dog show take place?

43. What does ASCOB mean?

44. What is a "major"?

45. When showing your dog in the ring should you go clockwise or counter-clockwise around the ring?

46. What do you mean if you say, "My dog got a HIT today"?

47. The AKC held its prestigious Centennial Dog Show in November 1984. What dog won Best in Show?

48. William Kendrick was the Best in Show judge at the Centennial Dog Show. What is his nickname?

49. Dog fanciers think that Judge William Kendrick is predisposed to a certain color, thus if they wear it in the ring it will bring good luck. What is this color?

50. AKC stands for what?

51. What are the two acceptable adult Poodle trims in the show ring?

52. Which is an acceptable show coat for the Puli, brushed out or corded?

53. If a judge comments about the flicking pasterns of your show dog, should you take this as a compliment?

54. What two separate breeds can be registered as such instead of as two varieties within one breed, following March 1, 1985, AKC approval?

55. When the handler drops the lead during a TDX trial, where is he usually standing?

56. What does it mean if your dog is "finished"?

57. Who was America's first woman dog show judge?

58. What is the oldest dog magazine in the US?

59. Which of these exercises are worth forty points toward a perfect 200 score in the Novice Obedience Class?
    a) Heel on leash
    b) Heel free
    c) Recall

60. The Kentucky Derby is the oldest consistently held sporting event in the United States. What is the second oldest?

61. Some show exhibitors "chalk" their dogs. Why do they do this?

62. If your dog is entered in a Bermuda conformation show, will he need a "major" to receive a championship there?

63. How many points do you need to win Canada's highest title of champion?

64. What exercises in the obedience trial Novice Class are done with a group of handlers and dogs?

65. Name three breeds accepted by the AKC in the Miscellaneous Class at shows.

66. How many points must a dog accumulate to become a breed champion in Australia?

67. The Sporting Group and the Hound Group consist of hunting dogs. What is the difference in the game they pursue?

68. Who was considered the only official AKC photographer?

69. As of January 1, 1984, three new breeds became eligible for AKC registration. Name them.

70. To register your dog in Canada you must either tattoo it or do what to it?

71. How many breeds are in the Working Group?

72. How many breeds does the AKC accept in the Hound Group?

73. The Non-Sporting Group is the smallest of the AKC classifications. How many breeds are in this group?

74. Which exercise in Open Classes of obedience trials is worth forty points?

75. Following what type of tracks causes the tracking dog to fail?

76. What woman was most instrumental in getting the AKC to recognize and approve the sport of dog obedience?

77. What was her favorite breed?

78. In what month is the Westminster Kennel Club Show held?

79. What is the purpose of the figure eight in Novice Obedience exercises?

80. Ch. St. Aubrey Dragonora of Elsdon, a Pekingese, won Best in Show at the 1982 Westminster Kennel Club Show. What did her handler carry her in after she won the show?

81. Who was her handler?

82. How many Border Collies have received the title of champion at AKC conformation shows?

83. Where is the second flag in a tracking dog test?
    a) Forty yards from the first
    b) Twenty yards from the first
    c) Thirty yards from the first

84. Would a tracking dog be looking for ducks or would its handler be wearing them?

85. Is a dog that is "paddling along" actually in the water?

86. When was the first Westminster Kennel Club Show held?

87. Where was it held?

FOR THE EXPERT

1. What two breeds have double dewclaws on their hind legs?

2. The United Kennel Club is the largest register of what kind of dogs?

3. What is the rarest breed in the world and the only surviving aboriginal dog of North America?

4. Approximately how many of these dogs are thought to be in existence?

5. Name the great Smooth Fox Terrier of the late 1930s that won almost everything except the Garden.

6. What German rescue dog, which the AKC does not accept, has webbed feet?
    a) Neapolitan Mastiff
    b) Leonberger
    c) Hovawart

7. What is the largest recorded litter of puppies?

8. Who was the first president of the American Kennel Club (AKC)?

9. The Doberman Pinscher comes in black, blue and fawn. What's another name for the fawn?
    a) Hindenburg
    b) Isabella
    c) Appolina

10. How many toes does a dog's forefoot have?

11. To what do Bijou, Tantivy, Skycastle and Timber Ridge refer?

12. What are the two types of Corgis?

13. In Australia, if a sheepdog is "backing" a flock of sheep, what is it doing?

14. If your dog has ringworm, is a species of worm involved?

15. Asra, Omar and Badslu formed the cornerstone of what breed in the US?

16. What breed was the AKC's first Champion of Record?

17. How many breeds are recognized by the Canadian Kennel Club?

18. What does it mean when an Australian Shepherd is said to have "ghost eyes"?

19. A number of dogs have webbed feet. Name three.

20. What is the principal difference between the Irish standard and the American standard for the Kerry Blue Terrier?

For the Expert

21. What is generally considered the period of gestation for a bitch?

22. Do Malamutes or Huskies frequently have blue eyes?

23. A tracking dog's leash should be how long?

24. The Aidi is practically unheard of outside of its north African country. Name this country.

25. In what Irish county were the "scarteen beagles" known for over 200 years?

26. If you had a Rafeiro do Alentejo, what would you do with it?

27. What are ultratrevilear dogs?

28. What are Tazys, Tajans and Chortajs?

29. What are the Bedlington Terrier's two distinct colors?

30. What's the normal temperature (°F) of an adult dog?
    a) 101-102.5
    b) 98.6-99
    c) 100-101

31. For what is the Tennessee Treeing Brindle noted?

32. According to the Bringsel method for Search-and-Rescue dogs, how does the dog let its handler know its made a find?

33. The Toy Manchester Terrier is a variety of the Manchester Terrier. Are they in the same group?

34. Each fall the Westchester Kennel Club holds its prestigious dog show at what famous estate?

35. In 1984 the US Postal Service issued four stamps honoring American dogs. What breeds were honored?

36. How many breeds are recognized by the Australian National Kennel Council?

37. Collies used to have a "tortoise shell" color. What is this color called today?

38. Should you be happy if your Pointer is considered a "blinker"?

39. You've packed your tents, family and dogs and have moved from southern Afghanistan to the northern regions; how does your hound look different from his new friends?

40. If someone refers to the "trousers" of a dog, to what is the person referring?

41. What unusual breed has a coat (as its name suggests) of long, heavy, cotton-like white hair and is a native of southern Madagascar?

42. What is Tetralogy of Fallot?

43. Only one Tibetan breed has a hare foot instead of the cat or round foot. Name this breed.

44. In addition to the hairless dogs native to Mexico, there is a hairless breed native to China. Name this breed.

45. If your dog got "spiked," did he step on a rusty nail?

46. Lovers of what breed recognize 1920s English Champion Sirdar of Ghazni as one of their own?

47. What breed, which originated in the jungles of Malaysia, may be the link between the Dingo and Basenji?

48. This breed is named after what?

49. Although a dog's eyesight is sharp, dogs often cannot distinguish details at the same distance as the human eye can. What accounts for this difference?

50. Which is the largest Spaniel?

51. According to the AKC, what breed of dog is more popular than the Poodle?

52. If you were at a dog track and someone said the race was won by a "gyp," would you think that someone had cheated?

53. Which of the following is not a member of the canis family: the coyote, fox or wolf?

54. Which one of these breeds is not a member of the Herding Group?
    a) Komondor
    b) Bearded Collie
    c) Belgian Tervuren
    d) Puli

55. How do the following terms refer to dog breeds: Braccoids, Graiods, Lupoids and Molossoids?

56. Of the approximately 400 dog breeds in the world, how many are recognized by the American Kennel Club?

57. How many toes does a dog's hind foot have?

58. According to the AKC, which breed of dog had the fewest registrations for 1984?

59. How many teeth are on the upper jaw of an adult dog? The lower?

60. Name two breeds that can be "corded."

61. Someone comments that your dog is suffering from papillomatosis; does this mean it is in love with a little "butterfly dog"?

62. What dog has been called the "Louisiana hawg dawg," "Swamp dog" and "Calcutter cur"?

63. New Zealand sheepherders use two types of herding dogs. What do they call them?

64. Which type barks and which type doesn't bark?

65. What is the difference between a hypermetric and a elliptometric dog?

66. What does "box broken" mean in the coursing world?

For the Expert

67. What is the small hook at the end of a dog's tail called?

68. What breed is considered the Czechoslovakian National Hound?

69. What is the FCI?

70. For what are Bongo of Blean and Bokoto of Blean noted?

71. What is Cushing's Syndrome?

72. How many teeth do puppies grow after birth?

73. What are the coat types of Dachshunds?

74. Name the ancient breed of dog, considered to be the progenitor of the Chihuahua, which was a favorite of the Aztecs.

75. How much larger an area do the olfactory (smell) membranes of a dog take up in comparison to a man's?
    a) 10 to 100 times
    b) 100 to 1000 times
    c) 1000 to 10,000 times

76. What 19th century Australian cattle dog was a cross between the Dingo and the Smithfield?

ANSWERS

GENERAL

1. Snoopy

2. Greyfriar's Bobby

3. Hartsdale, New York

4. Helen Keller

5. The Monks of New Skete

6. No, unless you want to eat an Italian breed of dog for dessert

7. Going into space

8. "Barker"

9. Buddy

10. Dalmatian

11. No, it's a shoal in the North Sea.

12. The dog begins a fight by using his front paws.

13. No, a stray calf

14. RCA

15. **His Master's Voice**

16. Francis Barraud

17. Nipper

18. The original painting depicted a cylinder phonograph; he repainted it as a disc phonograph.

19. A sailor. A doghouse is a small cabin with a high profile.

20. No, a "sharp" dog shows signs of emotional instability and might attack without provocation.

21. Small

22. The dogwood

23. Beans

24. During the voyage of Noah's Ark, holes in the vessel were supposedly plugged with dogs' noses.

25. Thirteen

26. Promoting the use of dogs by the deaf

27. Possibly, but this could also refer to ruthless competition conducted without any self-restraint

28. The Bulldog

29. No, a stop is the depression or step-down in the topline of the head, between the eyes.

General - Answers

30. Komondor

31. Idaho (some 10,500 years old)

32. The Bluegrass Open Sheep Dog Trials, held in Lexington, Kentucky

33. For saving a place in a book (by folding back a page corner)

34. Elvis Presley

35. No, most likely the person means leave well enough alone.

36. "How Much Is that Doggie in the Window?"

37. "Dogfight"

38. No, it's a small weather vane found on a ship.

39. A night so cold it takes three dogs, acting as blankets, to keep a person warm

40. Bingo

41. Paul Bunyan

42. Between July and September, when the dog star Sirius can be seen in the skies

43. Yukon King

44. Silver King

45. The Waterloo Cup

46. Jim, the Wonder Dog

47. When you can walk around barefooted

48. From the Latin "terra," meaning earth (Terriers dig after burrowing prey.)

49. Packs of hounds receive a blessing.

50. Bob Dylan, on the album "New Morning"

51. Hachiko accompanied his master to the train each morning, returning each afternoon to greet him. His master died at work one day, but Hachiko continued the daily trip alone until his death nine years later.

52. The US dog stamps

53. A wager

54. She's putting her tail to one side, indicating that she's ready to be bred.

55. No, you're going to lower class dog tracks.

56. Red Rover

57. Barbara Woodhouse

58. No, your dog has tan spots on its cheeks and over its eyes.

59. They assume an attitude of wealth or importance.

60. A dog food manufactured by the Iams Company.

61. England

62. Dog Cakes and Mange Cure; "Spratts Patent, Limited"

63. The US Marines

64. No, it means he has gone into hiding.

65. a) John Muir

66. Prince

67. Spot

68. No, you've lost your leash.

69. b) Rabid dogs in the cities

70. Kal Kan

71. No, "wearing" means the Sheepdog is moving from side to side behind a flock in order to keep the flock together and in a straight line.

72. McGruff, the Bloodhound

73. Hushpuppies

74. He's referring to the dog's mental sense.

75. The Gaines Fido

76. c) He was stuffed and sent to the Carnegie Museum in Pittsburgh.

77. Frisbee or disc-catching

78. The golfer has just made a shot that turns at a sharp angle.

79. Rudolph Valentino

80. The hindquarters, from hip to stifle

81. 1859, in England

82. Ashley Whippet

83. a) The owner was jailed, and the dog was lost.

84. The letter 'R,' especially when trilled, because of its resemblance to a dog's growl

85. Maida, a Scottish Deerhound

86. Six

87. No, they pant and water evaporates from their mouths to cool their bodies.

88. **Canis familiaris**

89. Jan van Lawick-Goodall

90. Richard Burton and Elizabeth Taylor

91. The hot dog

92. Because dog flesh is eaten in these places

93. Boo

94. The North Carolina State basketball team

95. Xavier Cugat

96. Chihuahua

97. Llasa, Tibet

General - Answers

98. Three

99. 1) Canis Major—the great dog
    2) Canis Minor—the little dog
    3) Canis Venatici—the hunting dogs

100. b) The dog wagged its tail horizontally or perpendicularly.

101. To the right

102. Hawaii

103. England, in 1832 (the US in 1866)

104. German Shepherds, Golden Retrievers and Labrador Retrievers

105. The OFA (Orthopedic Foundation for Animals, Inc.)

106. By examining the dog's radiograph (x-ray)

107. Approximately every two weeks

108. New York City ($100)

109. His tail has been cut, and thus permanently shortened.

110. Twenty-nine years and five months, in Australia

111. With you

112. Barking a lot

113. The Cairn should weigh a stone.

114. No, he is standing watch on either the 4-6 p.m. or 6-8 p.m. shift.

115. Viral pneumonia

116. A harness

117. Purina

118. Buster Brown

119. He will approach the sheep.

120. Irish Setter (red, and red and white)
     Irish Terrier
     Kerry Blue Terrier
     Irish Water Spaniel
     Irish Wolfhound

121. Cerberus

122. Fear of dogs

123. An Army uniform

124. Bear baiting with Mastiff fighting dogs.

125. No, you are utterly exhausted or worn out.

126. b) Tail wagging

127. Scottie and Westie

128. In the center of a white blaze on the top-skull between the ears

129. A mistake has been made.

130. Ogden Nash

131. b) Dachshund

132. Moon Doggie

133. One hundred years of AKC history

134. Junkyard Dog

135. No, this refers to ears with a slight forward curvature.

136. Ten

137. About twenty

138. Probably forty million, dating back to the Oligocene Period

139. The Bulldog

140. Dog sled racing

141. Hill's Science Diet

142. Dogbane, which has medicinal properties (Wolfbane is quite poisonous.)

143. PAT (Puppy Aptitude Test)

144. You are likely to get bitten by a dog with rabies.

KNOW YOUR
BREEDS

1. Shih Tzu

2. He could be, but he also might be talking about a Norwegian scenting hound called the Dunker.

3. Norwich Terrier

4. Truffles

5. Rhodesian Ridgeback

6. Great Pyrenees, Kuvaszok, and Komondorok

7. Red and white

8. Great Dane

9. Norfolk Terrier

10. "A lot of dog in a small space"

11. Bedlington Terrier

12. b) The Yorkshire Terrier is a member of the Toy Group.

13. White English Terrier

14. Old English Sheepdog

15. Bloodhound

16. No, they are three separate and distinct breeds that (for the most part) developed independently of each other.

17. The Portuguese Water Dog

18. Airedale

19. a) The Welsh Corgi, which is a member of the Herding Group

20. Chihuahua

21. Molera

22. White Bull Terrier

23. Staffordshire Terrier

24. Siberian Husky

25. Weimaraner

26. Collie and Shetland Sheepdog

27. Irish Terrier

28. Because of its origins at the border between Scotland and England

29. Chocolate

30. Otter Hound

31.   For killing wolves

32.   Clumber Spaniel

33.   b) Sherwood Forest

34.   Yugoslavia

35.   Welsh Terriers

36.   Ruby Spaniel

37.   Greyhounds and Whippets

38.   Dalmatian

39.   Its bat ears

40.   c) The Tibetan Spaniel, which is a member of the Non-Sporting Group

41.   Newfoundland

42.   The Jura Laufhund, which is a member of the Swiss Laufhund family and also includes the Schweizer and Bernier Laufhunds

43.   Black, blue merle and sable

44.   Chihuahua

45.   No, a lurcher is a terrier-greyhound cross prized by British poachers.

46.   The steppes of the Southern Ukraine

47.   Dachshund

48.   Tibetan Terrier

49. Toy Poodle

50. Cardigan

51. Belgian Sheepdog

52. Chesapeake Bay Retriever

53. Dalmatian

54. Affenpinscher

55. Bearded Collie

56. Australian Cattle Dog

57. Brussels Griffon

58. Bernese, Greater Swiss, Entebuch and Appenzell

59. No, it refers to the patched or pied coloration of the Great Dane.

60. Dingo

61. Pharaoh Hound

62. Alsatian

63. Bearded Collies

64. Akita

65. Ibizans

66. It's a black and white Newfoundland.

67. Basset Hound

68. Weimaraner

69. Japanese Chins

70. Saluki

71. Basenji

72. It is Middle English for a fierce watchdog chained by day and released at night.

73. Chow Chow

74. Shar-Pei

75. a) It fastidiously cleans itself like a cat.

76. Bouvier des Flandres

77. Pembroke Welsh Corgi

78. Afghan

79. Colored

80. Boxer

81. Belgian Malinois, Belgian Tervuren

82. Whippet

83. The roach back

84. Irish Water Spaniel

85. No, the Doberman is a more recent breed created by Louis Doberman. The Miniature is several centuries old.

86. Bi-blues and bi-blacks

87. It's a hairless Mexican dog.

88.   Airedale Terrier

89.   Coonhounds

90.   Sicily

91.   Norway

92.   Pekingese

93.   English Setter

94.   Belgrave Joe, a Smooth Fox Terrier

95.   Great Pyrenees

96.   Gordon Setter

97.   Whippets

98.   Shorthaired

99.   Schipperke

100.   Butterfly and the nightmoth

101.   King Charles and Cavalier King Charles
       Spaniels

102.   Boston Terrier

103.   Bloodhound

104.   Pariah Dog

105.   English Cocker Spaniel

106.   To find the wounded and carry
       messages during military conflicts

107.   Irish Terrier

108. Basenji

109. Miniature Pinscher

110. China

111. "Monkey Dog"

112. Newfoundland

113. The first longhaired varieties appeared.

114. Bichon Frise or Teneriffe

115. "Low-set"

116. Pharoah Hound

117. Brazil

118. a) They died of distemper.

119. Lhasa Apso

120. Australian and Yorkshire Terriers

121. Brussels Griffon

122. Vizsla

123. Black, yellow and chocolate

124. Irish Setter

125. a) Cocker Spaniel

126. Wirehaired Pointing Griffon

127. Barbet

128. Off the coast of Spain in the west Mediterranean Sea

129. France

130. No, a Border Collie is used for herding while a Komondor is a flock guard dog that wouldn't take very well to the Border Collie's activities.

131. Yugoslavia

132. Bull Mastiff

133. No, it might also be a dog club formed to promote the "billy" breed, a hunting dog.

134. Transylvanian Hound

135. Pinscher

136. Ridgeback

137. Alaskan

138. Collie

139. Dinmont

140. Coated

141. Retriever

142. Hound

143. Japanese

144. Blue

145. Apso

146. Pinscher

147. Norwegian

148. Water

149. Saint

150. Sheepdog

151. Tzu

152. Terrier

153. Wheaten

154. Staffordshire

155. Highland

156. Pointing

157. Tan

158. Frise

159. King Charles

160. Brussels

161. Chow

162. Welsh

163. Mountain

164. Belgian

DOGS IN HISTORY AND POLITICS

1. General George Patton

2. Barry

3. Moritz

4. Great Dane

5. Him

6. Winks, owned by FDR

7. Be careful—it means "Beware of the dog."

8. General Dwight D. Eisenhower

9. Alexander the Great

10. Ben Franklin

11. Lisette

12. The prints of King Arthur's Cabal

13. Tang. He saved the lives of several children by pulling them from the path of oncoming vehicles.

14. Rex

15. Probably not. This is a Toy Poodle.

16. **The Avesta**

17. a) Turvy

18. Gandi

19. a) Cupid

20. World War II

21. The Wilson and Harding administrations

22. Finn

23. a) Thoutou

24. US Marine Corps

25. Thomas Jefferson

26. At his feet

27. Peter Pan

28. Collie

29. Prudence Prim

30. Rob Roy

31. Chinooks (heavy, draft-type dogs)

32. St. Bernard

33. Otterhound

34. C. Fred Bush

35. Egypt

36. Jacqueline Kennedy

37. Switzerland

38. The lion

39. b) Yuki

40. White Collie

41. Charlemagne

42. She supposedly attacked an elephant, worrying its head and trunk so it fell to the ground.

43. A bronze statue

44. Genghis Khan

45. Marco Polo

46. c) Italian Greyhound

47. The Crusaders

48. Water

49. Maltese

50. General George Washington

51. Sandy of **Annie** fame

52. "Albert" is engraved on the lock. When you press 'A' the lock opens.

53. Hindus

54. He was killed by a car on the White House grounds.

55. Arrian

56. Irish Wolfhound

57. c) White

58. Lassie

59. John Adams

60. Great Pyrenees

61. Dogs for Defense

62. St. Dominic

63. He kept nipping the heels of White House employees.

64. Looty

65. A Cavalier King Charles Spaniel

66. China

67. Blancs de Rey or King's Whites

68. White

69. "Grey" hound laws

70. Poodles (Imperiales are small pointed beards on the underjaw.)

71. "Singing Beagles"

72. Kuvasz

73. a) Cutie

74. They detected mines.

75. They kept getting blown up by the mines they were trying to detect.

76. Pasha was the Yorkie, Vicky the Miniature Poodle.

77. Afghan

78. Old English Sheepdog

79. a) Davie

80. Poodle

81. J.F.K.'s Charlie. When not romancing a pretty little Russian, he loved to chase squirrels.

82. Probably the Mastiff

83. Athens

84. She was afraid the German soldiers would steal him because he was so pretty.

85. They were given healing baths in the fountain of naphtha.

86. Fleas

87. Iraq

88. Achilles

89. Fala

90. Lucky

91. At his feet

92. Herbert H. Lehman

93. Lyndon B. Johnson

94. Italian Greyhound

95. George Washington

96. b) He went and lay down at Gunnar's feet.

97. Dominicans

98. Anubis

99. English Toy Spaniel

100. Dutch

101. Kees de Gyslaer of Dordrecht, a Dutch patriot during the French Revolution

102. Balto

103. Checkers

104. a) Canute Laws

105. a) Cut the tendons of the dog at its hock

106. b) The owner had to pay ten pence for every mile nearer the forest.

107. Lyndon B. Johnson's J. Edgar, a Beagle. He received a second at the trial.

108. They were team members of the Byrd expedition to "Little America."

109. He tore a muscle in his shoulder and had to hobble the 400 miles back to "Little America" on three legs.

110. Gelert

111. His son hiding in a corner and a dead wolf

112. A stone cairn honoring Gelert

113. Riding (he was a Fox Terrier)

114. The dog was named after the hospice.

115. Garm

116. Penistone

117. Judas Iscariot

118. F.D.R.'s Fala, whose full name was Murray of Fallahill after Roosevelt's relatives the Murrays whose Scottish estate is known as Fallahill

119. Hecate

120. A Poodle

121. Distinguish a Christian from an infidel

122. Jeff

123. Irish Wolfhound

124. Heidi

125. Weimaraner

126. Queen Victoria

127. Louis XIV

128.   Cortes

129.   Henry VIII

130.   Queen Victoria

131.   Pugs

132.   The Mormons

133.   A military coat and cap

134.   King Tut

135.   Weegie

136.   **White House Pets**

137.   He bit a piece of meat, swallowed it, was wracked with seizure, gave a death rattle and fell to the ground. Applause revived the little fellow.

138.   Irish Setter

139.   She put secret messages under his collar.

140.   Pekingese

141.   Pekingese

142.   Julie Nixon Eisenhower

143.   Bulldog

144.   Chow Chow

145.   All of them

146. Pyrethrum

147. President Gerald Ford's

148. Yuki was found by family members at a filling station where he had been abandoned.

149. No, these dogs were used to help WWII vets recuperate, particularly from shell shock.

150. St. Patrick

151. In India

152. Don

153. Shih Tzu

154. It was jackal-headed and had a human body.

155. "I'm not a Golden Retriever."

156. **Tomarctus**

157. They took part in rabbit hunting activities with field hounds.

158. Beagles

159. "Sullivan's Hounds" (after Colonel John S. Sullivan, Commander of Camp Ellis, himself a dog fancier)

160. St. Guinefort

161. Beijing (Peking)

162. a) England
      b) Middle Ages
      c) Hunted deer or boar in the royal
         forest using a hound on a lead to
         track your quarry

163. All of them

164. Woodrow Wilson

165. Golden Retriever

166. Mastiffs

167. Large Mastiffs similar to those brought
      back from Persia and India by the
      Greeks

168. b) Gona

169. Pembroke Welsh Corgi

170. Asclepius

171. b) Wolf

DOGS IN ART AND LITERATURE

1. Tricki-Woo

2. Napping in the grass

3. The Poe were used exclusively for food by natives of Tahiti and the Sandwich Islands.

4. Border Collie

5. In their kennel (or dog house)

6. Eric Knight

7. Two, Malamutes

8. **Far From the Madding Crowd**

9. Pugs

10. Dorothy Parker

11. Bull Terrier and yellow Labrador

12. Loath and Badger

13. Mark Twain

14. Blenheim Spaniels

15. Albert Payson Terhune

16. a) **The Pioneer** and c) **The Prairie**

17. b) Natty Bumppo

18. The lady is sitting on a chair with the dog lying at her feet on an oriental rug.

19. Blue

20. They're drinking from a bowl.

21. b) Camp

22. c) Sir Walter Scott

23. Standard Schnauzer

24. b) A dog keeping vigil for three months over the body of its master, who fell from Mt. Helvellyn to his death

25. b) The harper

26. Center forefront with the hand of the Prince of Wales resting on his head

27. a) "An Elegy on the Death of a Mad Dog"

28. c) John Gay

29. b) Ali

30. a) Chris

31. He reverted to the wild and joined a wolf pack.

32. b) Dachshund

33. b) Nig

34. Two big champagne-colored Poodles

35. Folly and Buzz

36. Three

37. Cabal

38. A satire on the institution of marriage

39. Spitz

40. No, he's a fox.

41. Roy Andersen

42. King Edward VII

43. One of the little girls is sitting on him.

44. Landseer Newfoundland

45. **Black Marble**

46. Baron Munchausen

47. **The Plague Dogs**

48. Orph

49. In the reception room of the American Kennel Club

50. Painting horses, Hounds, Greyhounds and gun dogs

51. Fox Terriers

52. She whelps and has "enough hound/to go all around."

53. Albert Payson Terhune

54. **Every Night Josephine**

55. They remained silent.

56. Barbara Woodhouse

57. An Irish Setter puppy

58. In the tomb of King Antefaa II in the valley of El Assasif

59. White with red markings

60. French

61. Betty White

62. Barbara Woodhouse

63. Jip

64. Two

65. Fred Gipson

66. **Men, Women, and Dogs**

67. A dwarf is resting his foot on the dog's back.

68. b) is a displaced guard dog of a gulag.

69. Mexican Hairless (Pelon Dog)

70. A bandage. He'd had a brain operation, and the bandage covered the plate over his brain.

71. Mister Timber Doodle

72. Collie

73. Sir Walter Scott

74. The Greyhound

75. Pointers

76. Marcus Valerius Martalis

77. She waited for Joe Carraclough outside his school.

78. b) Boatswain

79. c) Newfoundland

80. He walked to him, touched his hand, fell down and died.

81. "The Hound of Heaven"

82. The dog found Ernest in Ketchum, Idaho.

83. Canis Major, especially the star Sirius

84. b) Bull's Eye

85. He jumped from the parapet from which Sikes had fallen, fell thirty-five feet, hit his head on a stone and died.

86. b) Pomero

87. So he would drown. The man couldn't pay the tax on his dog.

88. Grey brindle and brown brindle

89. That Man never existed

90. William Butler Yeats

91. Samuel Pepys

92. a) John Steinbeck

93. c) Douglas and Percy

94. Greyhound

95. Elizabeth Barrett Browning

96. **Flush**; Virginia Woolf

97. Noel Coward

98. Newfoundland

99. Fight other vicious dogs

100. He wore every tooth in his jaw down to the gums.

101. **The Poky Little Puppy**

102. Puppy dog tails

103. Cuchullain, which means Cullan's hound

104. Count Gaston Phoebus, who is said to have always traveled with an entourage of 1,600 dogs

105. Jonathan Swift

106. Dandie Dinmont

107. Duchess, the Pomeranian

108. Miniature Schnauzer

109. **Bob, Son of Battle**

110. It has a lion cut.

111. Mastiff, Whippet, and Setter

112. a) Maggie

113. Whippet

114. "Dalmatian Gus"

115. Black Dog or Blackie

116. Relieving himself

117. **Cujo**

118. Bonkers

119. Snitter and Roulf

120. a) Keeper

121. b) Queen

122. **The Hound of the Baskervilles**

123. Basket I and Basket II

124. Rex

125. He incriminated a man for the master's murder, did battle with him and won. The man was then hanged for the crime.

126. Bichon Frise

127.   Borzoi

128.   b) Charles le Chien

129.   Ares (Mars), the god of war

130.   a) Fred

131.   Hobo

132.   Dr. Johannes Caius (John Keyes)

133.   Shakespeare

134.   "Tristan and Isolt"

135.   Sir Edwin Landseer

136.   Mundo Cani Dog

137.   Hector his Jack Russell, and Dan his Labrador

138.   Robert Louis Stevenson

139.   Maurice Maeterlinck

140.   Beatrix Potter

141.   Bounce

142.   The Prioress

143.   A good gnawable beef bone

144.   The Lochs

145.   Bloodhounds

146.   Three bells and a big bow

147.   Mark Twain

148.   c) Fice, which means a small snappish dog

149.   c) **The Accidental Tourist**

150.   A pair of shoes

151.   Fourteen

152.   Carlo

153.   b) Lion

154.   A red bow

155.   Two Fox Terriers delivered a wounded Collie companion to the hospital to receive help.

156.   Under the banquet table

157.   Miss MacTavish; **The Kennel Murder Case**

158.   Fido

159.   Nana

160.   Scarlet

161.   Beauty Smith

162.   Five

163.   His name (Barbero)

164.   b) Trump

165.   b) John S. O'Brien

166.   b) He was beaten to death by a tramp.

PHOTOS

1. Bearded Collie

2. This is Champion Ballycastle's Blue Bear, the author's constant companion.

3. Togo

4. He was lead dog of the Serum Run that saved Nome, Alaska, from diptheria in 1925.

5. Lenhard Seppala

6. St. Hubert's Giralda Animal Welfare and Education Center

7. Geraldine Rockefeller Dodge

8. St. Francis

9. Ezio Pinza with Boris and Figaro

10. Dalmatians

11. Dogs for Defense

12. Lassie

13. **Lassie Come Home**

14. Joe Carraclough

15. Roddy McDowell

16. Ken-L Ration Show Dog of the Year

17. Ch. Warren Remedy, a Smooth Fox Terrier

18. Quaker Oats Company

19. Asta

20. Myrna Loy and William Powell

21. Dashiell Hammett

22. English Setter

23. Adonis

24. He was the first dog the AKC registered in its Stud Book.

25. Rin Tin Tin

26. **Frozen River**

27. 1932

28. Elizabeth Taylor

29. **The Courage of Lassie**

30. Rudd Weatherwax

31. Newfoundland

32. Landseer Newfoundland (after the painter Sir Edwin Landseer)

33. Its feet are webbed.

34. Steverino

35. "The Steve Allen Show"

36. Gary Moore

37. Abraham Lincoln

38. Fort Wayne, Indiana

39. Lincoln's great love of animals, especially dogs

40. The Dog Museum of America

41. On the main floor of AKC headquarters at 51 Madison Avenue, New York City

42. William Secord

43. Belgian Tervuren

44. Belgian Sheepdog

45. Belgian Malinois

46. Owney

47. Mascot of the Railway Mail Service

48. He traveled back and forth across America in post office railway cars. In 1895 he ended his career with an

around-the-world journey. He traveled aproximately 150,000 official miles in his lifetime.

49. The Long sit

50. From left to right: Chesapeake Bay Retriever, Bearded Collie and Irish Setter

51. Charlie and Pushinka

52. John F. Kennedy

53. Nikita Krushehev

54. They had four puppies.

55. Welsh Terrier

56. Beagle

57. Cinderella (Bridal Vale's Cinderella UDTX)

58. Cindy became the first TDX Beagle in Canada and the US.

59. Briard

60. Whooki (Ch. Brie-Zee Little Whooki, UDTX, Can. CDX, Can. TDX, FH). Whooki is the first and only Briard to hold the titles of Champion, Utility Dog and Tracking Dog Excellent. He is the first and only Briard to hold the Schutzhund FH, the German Advanced Tracking title conferred by NASA. Whooki is also a registered Therapy Dog, with a repertoire of about thirty parlor tricks.

61. Tracking

62. Bearded Collie

63. Am./Can. Ch. Cannamoor Honey Rose Am./Can. CD and TDX (Honey). Now departed, Honey was the first Beardie to receive a TD in both Canada and the US, the first and only Beardie to receive a TDX and the holder of more titles than any other Beardie.

64. Komondor

65. Aftscharka

66. Corded

67. Sporting Group
Hound Group
Working Group
Terrier Group
Toy Group
Non-Sporting Group
Herding Group

68. a) Dog #1 exhibits strong aggression.
b) Dog #3 exhibits a fearful posture.
c) Dog #2 exhibits an aggressive but also fearful demeanor.

69. Dog #1

70. 1. d) Gay tail
2. b) Tail with a frou-frou or pompom
3. a) Fox-brush with sickle curve
4. c) Docked tail
5. e) Ringed tail
6. f) Plumed tail

71. 1. c) Bat ear
2. a) Cropped ear

3. e) Button ear
4. f) Semi Prick ear
5. b) Hanging ear
6. d) Prick ear

72. Number 2 is the English Saddle, number 1 is the Continental.

73. The Sporting clip

74. Standard, Miniature and Toy

75. Apricot

MEDIA DOGS

1. Pete

2. Toto, in **The Wizard of Oz**

3. No, he was shot to put him out of his misery.

4. Krypto

5. Cocker Spaniel

6. Bullet

7. c) Muffey and Rink

8. **101 Dalmatians**

9. Cleo

10. Basset Hound

11. Irish Wolfhound

12. Snow

13. **Straw Dogs**

14. Poco

15. John Troy

16. The right eye

17. Chipper

18. Ladadog

19. Waldo

20. Muffin

21. Simone

22. Gin-Gin

23. Max

24. German Shepherd

25. Snuffy

26. Oregano

27. "The Love Boat," which featured a dog show as a two hour special

28. Tundra

29. Bernardo Barkalotte

30. Nubbin, a Redbone Hound

31. Doug

32. Dino

33. Floppy

34. Topper

35. Neil

36. Martinis

37. Buck

38. Nelson

39. Tramp

40. Jeff Miller

41. Timmy Miller

42. Pal

43. Fort Apache

44. Rusty

45. Texas

46. Brandon

47. **A Boy and His Dog**

48. a) Bull Terriers

49. Spike

50. Tiger (of "The Brady Bunch")

51. Bandit

52. Little Orphan Annie

53. A footman

54. Dagwood and Blondie

55. "Snuffy Smith"

56. Bulldog

57. Augie Doggie

58. Old English Sheepdog

59. Fred Basset

60. "Dennis the Menace"

61. Kip

62. Great Dane

63. Fifi

64. Snoopy, a Beagle

65. Brain

66. On his ears, back and the base of his tail

67. Spike

68. Afghan Hound

69. Old Yeller

70. Long coat

71. Lord Nelson

72. Border Terrier

73. Boomer

74. Muffit

75. Astro

76. Odie

77. Yuk

78. A doghouse

79. **Big Red**

80. Dingbat

81. A werewolf

82. Barfy

83. **Lady and the Tramp**

84. Snert

85. Irish Water Spaniel

86. Maria

87. Bimbo

88. Spike and Tyke

89. Bulldogs

90. **Dog Day Afternoon**

91. Mighty Manfred

92. Otto

93. He has a tooth that sticks out of his mouth.

94. Great Dane

95. Scooby is Scrappy's uncle.

96. Borzoi

97. Underdog

98. Goofy

99. Huckleberry Hound

100. Boo-Boo

101. Freeway

102. Belle

103. Australian Cattle Dog

104. A red bandana

105. Jip

106. Bonnie Jean

107. Roger Caras

108. "The Puppy's New Adventures"

109. Strongheart

110. Copper

111. Mr. Peabody

112. Duke, a Bloodhound

113. Benji

114. Pluto

115. Einstein

116. Buddy, the first American Seeing Eye Dog

117. **The Dogs of War**

118. He is a tiny puppy who eventually grows larger than people.

119. Buster and Oscar

120. Dotty Dog

121. Scamp

122. Caesar

123. Jasper

124. Deputy Dawg

125. Cap'n Bulldog

SHOW DOGS

1. The dog is a Conformation Champion, has an Obedience title of Companion Dog, and has received the highest award in scent tracking.

2. You would be at England's largest dog show.

3. Dogs must remain on public view in partitioned stalls for all or part of the day.

4. George Francis Foley

5. No, your dog has completed the three "legs" required for an obedience title.

6. Morris and Essex Kennel Club Show

7. Super Chief aka Soupy

8. Pairs of dogs competing by sex

9. You're making a smooth pivot in front of the judge before you gait your dog in the pattern the judge has requested.

10. New York

11. New England Dog Training Club

12. Four

13. Pointing dogs, scenting and trail hounds, retrievers, and flushing dogs

14. An advance notice detailing a forthcoming dog show

15. b) Ten

16. Any breed

17. No, and if you did your dog would never get its championship. It means a foolish, blundering official.

18. Eyeglasses

19. A dog must select from among identical articles which have its handler's scent.

20. Vizsla

21. Tracking

22. As soon as he is leash-trained

23. Robert Griffing

24. You have qualified for a leg at an obedience trial.

25. Geraldine Rockefeller Dodge

26. Thirteen inches and fifteen inches (at the shoulder)

27. King Charles and Ruby

28. Ear cropping

29. The person who will show your dog in the ring

30. Herding

31. Left

32. A dog that wins most of its points in smaller shows in outlying areas, requiring the use of a lot of petrol in traveling the great distances to attend such shows.

33. Fifteen

34. Left arm

35. Patterns for moving dogs

36. Ch. Rancho Dobe's Storm (1952 and 1953)

37. Seven

38. Golden Retriever

39. Field and Conformation

40. Brittanys

41. Black and Tan, ASCOB, and Parti-color

42. Quebec City, Canada in 1867

43. Any solid color other than black

44. A show dog that receives three to five points at a single show

45. Counterclockwise

46. The dog received High in Trial, which is considered the Obedience Best in Show.

47. Ch. Covy Tucker Hills Manhattan

48. "Wild Bill"

49. Green

50. American Kennel Club

51. Continental and English Saddle

52. Both

53. No, the judge is talking about a fault involving extremely loose movement of the dog's lower forelegs.

54. Smooth Fox Terrier and Wire Fox Terrier

55. In the woods

56. It has achieved points necessary to be designated champion.

57. Anna H. Whitney

58. **American Kennel Gazette**

59. a) Heel on Leash and b) Heel free

60. The Westminster Kennel Club Show

61. To whiten and give texture to a dog's coat

62. Yes

63. Ten (under three different judges)

64. The long sit and the long down

65. Any three of the following: Australian Kelpies, Border Collies, Cavalier King Charles Spaniels, Finnish Spitz, Miniature Bull Terrier and Spinoni Italiani

66. One hundred, including four Challenge Certificates

67. Sporting—feathered game
Hounds—mammals

68. Rudolph W. Tauskey

69. 1) Portuguese Water Dog
2) Pharaoh Hound
3) Tibetan Spaniel

70. Have a noseprint done

71. Nineteen

72. Twenty-one

73. Thirteen

74. Heel free

75. Crosstracks

76. Helene Whitehouse Walker

77. Poodle

78. February

79. To prove that the dog doesn't get tangled with passers-by even when weaving in and out of crowds

80. The trophy bowl

81. Bill Trainor

82. None, at this time the Border Collie is limited to the Miscellaneous Class and is thus ineligible for AKC championships.

83. c) Thirty yards from the first

84. The handler would be wearing them (ducks are the preferred footwear of trackers).

85. No, this is a gaiting fault (so named for its similarity to the motion of a canoeist's paddle).

86. May 1877

87. Gilmore's Garden, sometimes known as the Hippodrome

FOR THE EXPERT

1. Briard and Great Pyrenees

2. Coonhounds

3. Tahltan Bear Dog

4. Six

5. Nornay Saddler

6. c) Hovawart

7. Twenty-three pups (once by a Saint Bernard and once by a Foxhound)

8. Major James A. Taylor

9. b) Isabella

10. Five, counting the toe pad of the dew claw

11. They are names of Basset Hound packs.

12. Pembroke and Cardigan

13. Running across the sheep's backs in order to get to the leader when the flock is confined

14. No. Despite its name, ringworm does not involve worms. It is a fungus that grows under the skin.

15. Afghan

16. Beagle (Sir Novice)

17. 152

18. It has eyes of different colors (such as one brown and one blue).

19. Any three of the following: Portuguese Water Dog, Chesapeake Bay Retriever, Poodle, Labrador Retriever, Newfoundland and Hovawart

20. The Irish do not permit the trimming of the coat.

21. Approximately sixty-three days

22. Huskies

23. Between twenty and forty feet in length

24. Morocco

25. Kerry

26. You'd probably use him as your guard dog while living in Portugal.

27. Dogs with naturally short tails, such as the Bulldog

28. Breeds of ancient and endangered Russian sighthounds

29. Liver and blue

30.   a) 101-102.5

31.   For its persistent and sometimes successful attempts to climb trees in order to seize its prey

32.   The dog puts the bringsel (a sausage shaped device attached to a collar) in its mouth and returns it to the handler.

33.   No, the Manchester Terrier is in the Terrier Group and the Toy variety is in the Toy Group.

34.   Lyndhurst, in Tarrytown, New York

35.   Beagle, Boston Terrier, Chesapeake Bay Retriever, American Cocker Spaniel, Alaskan Malamute, Collie, Black and Tan Coonhound, American Foxhound

36.   130

37.   Blue merle

38.   Not particularly, since a blinker is a dog that points a bird and then leaves it, or one that doesn't make a definite point in the first place.

39.   The Afghan Hounds of the south are rangy, light in color and sparse of outer coat. The northern dogs are compact, dark and have heavy coats.

40.   The longish hair on the back thighs of some beeds

41.   The Coton De Tulear

42. A canine heart problem involving both narrowing of the pulmonary artery and a hole in the wall between the two heart chambers

43. Tibetan Spaniel

44. Chinese Crested Dog

45. No, he's a racing dog who's been injured by the claws of a following contestant.

46. Afghan

47. Telomanian

48. The Telom River

49. Dogs, like most other non-primate mammals, do not have a fovea, which is a small section of the retina not covered by blood vessels.

50. Clumber Spaniel

51. Cocker Spaniel

52. No, a gyp is a female Greyhound.

53. The fox (vulpes)

54. a) The Komondor is a member of the Working Group.

55. They describe the shape of a dog's head, which is one method used to classify dogs.

56. 128

57. Four

58. Harrier

59. Upper—twenty
    Lower—twenty-two

60. Any two of the following: Puli, Poodle
    and Komondor

61. No, it means its mouth is covered with
    benign warts.

62. Catahoula leopard cowdog

63. Headers and huntaways

64. The headers never bark, the huntaways
    always bark.

65. Height (A hypermetric is very tall, while
    a elliptometric dog is of the toy variety.)

66. A Greyhound trained to use a starting
    box.

67. Crochet

68. Black Forest Hound

69. The Federation Cynologique Interna-
    tionale (an international federation of
    national dog clubs not well-known in
    English-speaking countries)

70. Producing the first litter of Basenji's out-
    side Africa

71. A skin disease in which the adrenal
    glands produce too much of the cortisol
    hormone

72. Twenty-eight

73. Smooth, long and wirehaired

74. Techichi

75. c) 1,000 to 10,000 times

76. The Timmins biter, which went out of favor because of its excessive biting habits

Photo Credits

Archives of the International Siberian Husky Club
John F. Kennedy Library
Smithsonian Institution
Joan Ludwig
Robert Parsons
Robert K. Berry
Museum of Modern Art/Film Stills Archives
Gaines Dog Research Center
Grant Taylor
Ken-L Ration
New Bedford Standard Times
American Kennel Club Library